CW01020711

Retail Sales
&
Customer
Service

– Volume 1

CARLO G SANTORO

DEDICATION

This book is dedicated to all the future happy customers that are going to buy from you!

CONTENTS

ACKNOWLEDGMENTS

This book came about from years of watching and working with amazing retailers and inspiring people…..Thank you for all the knowledge you imparted.

I thank Sandy Newman for all her hard work and support in putting this book together.

I also thank my family: Debra, Silvia and Romeo.

FORWARD

Most retailers have a dynamic and diverse mix of staff in their stores, but have a single, common need from all of them – exceptional customer service.

If you are employed in a retail environment, do you know what it takes to give great customer service? Retail Sales & Customer Service Training – Volumes 1 and 2 - are a comprehensive guide to the fundamentals of why great customer service is so important, and how it can be achieved.

In an easy-to-read format, these books will take you through a logical progression from the basic principles of customer service and working in a retail environment, to your role on the shop floor. You will learn selling techniques; how to build a relationship with your customers, and numerous ways that you can work towards future sales. Full-timers, part-timers, casuals, people returning to the workforce or those of you in your first working role after leaving school or college will all benefit from the in-depth knowledge that these books will give.

We will look at the role of a salesperson in its entirety - from what to expect in a retail environment; the importance of product knowledge; how to present yourself; behaviour and body language and how to set goals for the future, through to stepping onto and actually working on the shop floor. You will be taught how to ask open and closed questions; to listen to the customer; learn how to overcome objections and close the sale; deal with complaints handling; store security; phone manner and competitive analysis, as well as successful sales techniques to use as tools. Even otherwise sensitive topics such as personal hygiene and body piercings are covered, to provide you with full coverage of what constitutes great customer service and how it can benefit both the company that you work for and your own career.

Volume 1 - *Sales Principles & Fundamental Concepts of Customer Service* - is designed to assist workers just like you, employed in a retail sales or service environment, at an entry or team member level.

This volume explores the importance of sales and good customer service in Retail and outlines the basic principles associated with such a role. Gaining a full understanding of these principles and concepts before venturing out onto the sales floor will not only make a job in this field easier for you to grasp, but will help lay the foundations to a successful career in a range of retail sales and customer service roles.

In Volume 1, fundamental principles such as product knowledge, store presentation and understanding basic retail formulae are explained, together with how factors such as body language and personal hygiene can affect the success of a sale. Occupational health and safety, competitor analysis and working as part of a team are also covered, as well as exploring cultural differences in a retail environment.

Volume 2: *Performing Retail Sales & Customer Service* will then move on to various sales techniques - outlining why a particular method is used and how this is advantageous in a selling environment – with sections on advanced techniques such as value-add selling and positive pitching. A comprehensive guide to Point of Sale (POS) is also covered.

So what are you waiting for? Let's get started!

VOLUME 1: SALES PRINCIPLES & FUNDAMENTAL CONCEPTS OF CUSTOMER SERVICE

CARLO G SANTORO

1. SELF-DEVELOPMENT & YOUR CAREER

"Success isn't a result of spontaneous combustion. You must set yourself on fire."

Arnold H Glasgow – Author and American humorist

Self-Development

In this chapter, you will learn the importance of self-development in setting you on the path for success, whatever your chosen career may be. Self-development is learning and growing; improving and developing new skills and potential, and leads to greater success in life. Understanding exactly who you are – what type of person you think you are; what you want to achieve in your life; what your strengths and weaknesses may be etc – and being open to learning & improving, helps you to grow and develop as a person and achieve great things. Self-development is vital to enable you to learn new skills and move forward in life, and is particularly important in terms of your career. Without self-development, quality of life and career prospects could be very limited, leading to a very dull existence.

The key factors in self-development include:

- improving self-awareness and self-knowledge
- building or renewing your identity
- developing strengths or talents
- identifying or improving potential
- improving employability or career potential
- enhancing lifestyle or the quality of life
- realising dreams
- fulfilling aspirations

Thinking about self-development and to help you understand a bit more about what type of person you are and what types of things you may want to achieve in your life, here's something that you might like to try:

* Jot down 10 things – any types of things at all - that you would really like to STOP doing and 10 things that you would really like to START doing and see if you can find a pattern or a common thread....

Your Career

Whatever type of industry you choose to work in, decisions that you make regarding your career are some of the most important that you will ever make. Your career is what will provide you with a way to make a living - to put a roof over your head; to put food on the table; to enable you to buy things like a car or a house; to allow you to travel or have nice clothes; and possibly to provide for a family.

Throughout your working life, you are embarking on a journey or a path – you may have heard of the term 'career path'? This generally refers to your path from leaving school and joining the workforce – possibly after studying in a specific field – and progressing through the many different stages in your career until you eventually retire. A career path may take you from a junior or apprentice in an organisation, through to a senior management position in later years. This progression, however, won't come about by itself.

Dedication to your role, integrity and hard work will help bring about promotions and financial rewards.

Throughout your career, it is in your best interest to be the best employee that you possibly can and to take your career seriously.

To do this may involve:
- a never ending thirst for knowledge
- always displaying honesty and integrity
- being an active team player
- respecting senior management
- being innovative and resourceful

You may, of course, opt to change careers along the way as you grow as a person and develop new skills and new interests. These days, not everyone ends up retiring in the same industry in which they started out. Sometimes, too, one career will set the foundations for another one to be born. Whatever career path you take, it should be fulfilling and rewarding and most importantly – enjoyable!

Goals & Aspirations

Everyone has wants and aspirations but not everyone sets themselves actual goals to achieve them. Goals are very important in both your personal and your working life. Setting goals helps you plan your future and gives you something definite to work towards. Reaching your goals is very rewarding. It gives you a great sense of achievement, which is positive and uplifting. This, in turn, gives you incentive to set further goals to achieve more from your life.

Goal setting is literally spelling out a specific achievement that you wish to attain, or a position that you would like to be in by a certain period of time. Time frames are important in setting yourself goals and both should be realistic. It is no good setting you goals that are vastly unachievable or impossible to achieve in the given time frame. This defeats the whole purpose of setting the goals in the first place. A time frame 'keeps it real', and gives you an exact target to aim for.

You can set yourself goals that are 'short-term' – that is, goals that you hope to achieve in the very near future – or you may set yourself some 'long-term' goals, which are usually bigger achievements and will take a bit longer to attain. Often a mixture of these two is used when setting yourself goals for both your personal and your professional life.

For example, you may set yourself goals that are very similar to or vastly different from some of the following lists.

Personal goals you might set could include:
- Travel to Europe in the next 18 months
- Learn to speak Italian in time for my trip
- Take my lunch to work instead of buying it, to save money – starting this week
- Walk to work twice a week instead of taking the tram – starting next week
- Donate to a charity each quarter

Whereas some professional goals you may want to achieve could include:
- Be promoted in my role in the next 12 months
- Increase my salary by 20% in the next year
- Improve my team management and delegation skills to assist with my promotion goal
- Undertake some part-time study in sales & marketing to assist with my role
- Practice my selling techniques to increase my ratio of closed sales

Can you see how some of these goals are 'short-term' goals and others are 'long-term' goals? It's also a good idea to review your goals and their time-frames from time to time to see if they are still relevant and achievable. You can also make new ones at any time – there aren't any rules involved.

When you have a minute, take the time to list your top 10 personal and professional goals that you hope to achieve over the next 12 months. You can refer to this list in months to come and see if your goals have changed at all and if you are on track to achieving them.

Mission, Vision & Values

Most organisations that you come across will have established their company's 'mission', 'vision' and 'values'. These are generally a set of guidelines or promises that the company endeavours to undertake and achieve to ensure the company's success.

- **Mission** defines the purpose of the company, why it exists and what it does to achieve its goals

- **Vision** is an intended future state - describing how the company would like to be

- **Values** are what the company stands for and the beliefs that are shared among the members of an organisation.

Defining Yours

Just as important as the company's mission, vision and values, however, are those that you set for yourself. It is important to know what your mission, vision and values are in life – both for your career and your personal life outside of work. Knowing clearly what these are will help you to plan for your future and achieve your goals.

Defining and establishing your mission, vision and values may appear challenging, but it shouldn't be. There are no right or wrong answers. You may also find that you have similar or vastly different definitions for those relevant to your personal life versus those relating to your career. Again, there is no right or wrong. The most important thing is that by outlining what your objectives are, it will assist you in achieving them.

Have you ever thought about what your **mission, vision** and **values** are for your personal life? And what do you think they might be for your career?

For example, as a salesperson, you might have a mission, a vision and values similar to the following:

- ➤ My **mission** is to be the best salesperson that I can, giving outstanding customer service to all my customers, always, to earn their trust and respect.
- ➤ My **vision** is to become a member of senior management and train others to become the best salespeople that they can be.
- ➤ My **values** are honesty, integrity, fairness and equality for all.

Make the effort and give it some serious thought. Defining your mission, vision and values is an invaluable exercise and well worth the time. You might be surprised at what you could learn about yourself!

"If you shoot for the stars and hit the moon, it's OK. But you've got to shoot for something. A lot of people don't even shoot."

Robert Townsend – Film director, writer, actor

2. SALES & CUSTOMER SERVICE

"A customer is the most important visitor on our premises. He is not dependent on us. We are dependent on him. He is not an interruption in our work. He is the purpose of it. He is not an outsider in our business. He is part of it. We are not doing him a favor by serving him. He is doing us a favor by giving us an opportunity to do so."

Mahatma Gandhi - Indian spiritual leader and activist

The Business Process

In this chapter, we will look at the reasons why sales and customer service are so important in the retail environment and how the two work hand in hand. Sales and customer service are really the crux or backbone of Retail, as without customer service, there would be very few sales and without sales, there would be no business.

In Retail, the process of engaging a customer and making a sale can be broken down into several basic systematic steps or actions. The following list shows the standard flow of the business process or sales process, using customer service to successfully make a sale. You will come across each of these steps and actions in more detail later in the book, so we won't go into detail on these just now.

Greet the customer

Approach (or reapproach)

Ask open and closed questions

Offer the solution

Close the sale

Thank the customer

The Business Purpose

There are key reasons behind a retail business being in operation – the obvious one being, to make money. Several significant business practices, however, are normally in place in a retail store's operation, to help make this happen. These practices are known as 'business purposes'. Business purpose may vary from store to store, but essentially, for a retail outlet, the principle business purposes will be very similar, and, if practiced correctly by the sales staff, all contribute to the store's potential to make money.

Some examples of key business purposes are as follows. These might be similar to those in place in your retail store:

To create new customers

To create great 'word of mouth'

To turn our customers into loyal supporters

To create repeat business

To enjoy what we do and who we work with

To increase brand awareness

The Importance of Customer Service

As a retail staff member, your job is to ensure that every customer has a welcoming and enjoyable experience in your store and that they leave your store with the right product or service for them. This is called customer service. Customer service involves greeting your customer, establishing their wants and needs and offering the appropriate solution. It may also involve follow-up after a sale or investigating a query prior to a sale. Overall, everything that you do to assist your customer in making a purchase is 'customer service'.

Good customer service is essential to make good sales and providing good customer service will help to build trust and rapport between you and your customers. This is important, as building trust and rapport will assist in not only maximising the potential for selling to a customer immediately, but also the potential for repeat business from the customer later down the track.

Using an Effective Greeting

When customers enter a retail store, they are expecting to be acknowledged promptly and in a friendly manner. Even if customers say they are "just looking", they must be acknowledged so they have been made aware that you know they are there. If you do not acknowledge the customers' presence, they will not feel welcome in your store, therefore minimising the potential for immediate or repeat business.

It is also important to be aware that customers from different cultures and different ethnic backgrounds will be used to different methods of greeting – depending on where they are from. For example, when introducing yourself to a customer, in Australia, sometimes it is appropriate to offer your hand in preparation for a handshake. In some cultures, this would not be understood and more importantly, could be seen as offensive.

The safest and most effective way to greet all customers, therefore, is to simply make eye contact with them and smile. Nodding at the same time is also effective and generally interpreted well by any culture. We will cover more on this topic in further chapters.

The Importance of Sales

A vital part of being a retail team member is sales. Sales are essential for a retail business to enable the business to make money. This is important simply because without money, there is no business.

To be a successful salesperson, you must ensure that you are asking the right questions to be able to match the right product or service to the customers' needs. This will not only help to make money for your business immediately, but the customer will trust you enough to return to your store for future business.

Small sales, too, are an important factor not to be overlooked. Several seemingly small sales can add up over the course of a day or a week and all help to make money for the business. More importantly, several sales versus one sale can mean several customers instead of just one. That also means several potential repeat customers instead of just one.

Increasing sales is a number one priority in all retail stores, so, for you as a salesperson and for the business in general, these are crucial factors to remember.

Repeat Business

Repeat business or a repeat customer is simply when a customer returns to your store to buy something again. Generally, they have been there at least once already, they were happy with what they bought or the service that they received, and they have come back to the store for more of the same.

Repeat business can become an income stream that is secure and guaranteed. It is much easier to sell to a current or repeat customer than it is to sell to a new customer, as they already have a degree of trust in you as a salesperson, making your job less difficult. It is vital, however, never to abuse this trust. Maintaining integrity with your repeat customers at all times, eventually makes them loyal customers. When customers become loyal customers, they are usually customers for life.

'Word of Mouth'

If a customer is happy with your product or the service that they received in your store, not only will they return as repeat clientele, chances are, they will tell someone they know. This transfer of information from person to person is known as word of mouth. Word of mouth referrals are an invaluable source of potential income for the business and a great asset to you as a salesperson.

Research shows that customers are more likely to visit a store and/or make a purchase if they were referred by word of mouth, than simply through a response to advertising. Be aware, however, that just as word of mouth in a positive sense can be advantageous to both you and the business, bad word of mouth can be disastrous. Evidently, significantly more word of mouth referrals are aired because of bad experiences than good ones; so, always ensure that you give customers a good experience to talk about.

Sales Targets & KPIs

As a salesperson, you will often be required to meet certain sales targets and KPIs.

Sales targets are an estimate or forecast of future sales that your organisation expects you to achieve within a given time frame. This could be short-term – i.e. a sales target per shift or per week; or longer-term – i.e. a sales target over a month or per quarter. Sales targets are generally based on previous figures for the same time frame (if available), or estimated using factors such as customer traffic numbers, ratio of staff to customers, popularity of products or services on offer, current advertising etc.

For example, a ladies' fashion store may have sold 73 red cashmere wraps last Winter season. This year, a heavy advertising campaign has been run for this item and stock levels are plentiful. A sales target of 150 or above may be set for this item based on the increased number of customers visiting the store daily, combined with the success of the current ad campaign.

KPIs or *Key Performance Indicators* are a measure of performance commonly used to help an organisation determine how successful it is in terms of making progress towards its long-term goals. Most companies will set down a list of KPIs for staff to work towards, which will assist the business in achieving specific goals or targets in a given time frame.

For example, in a retail store, a KPI might be: to increase the average spend per customer from $50.00 to $60.00 (i.e. by 20%) by the end of June the following year.

As a salesperson, you should be aware on a daily basis of any such KPIs in place in your business and work with your team to achieve them. It is important that you fully understand sales targets and KPIs and for you to discuss with your manager if you are unsure about them or are experiencing trouble meeting the required levels.

Other Key Elements of Sales & Customer Service

Other key elements to being a successful retail salesperson include:

- body language
- up-selling/cross-selling

- hand gestures
- tone of voice
- phone manner
- honesty

- shop presentation
- personal hygiene
- objection handling

These, and many more elements, make up the overall sales experience for the customer. If these elements are handled correctly, they will maximise the sales opportunity, effectively making more money for your business as well as maximising potential for repeat business. We cover each of these in more detail in future chapters.

Key Performance Indicators define a set of values used to measure against and usually follow the 'SMART' criteria. This is defined as follows:

the KPI has a **S**pecific purpose for the business

it is **M**easurable to really get a value of the KPI

the defined norms have to be **A**chievable

the KPI has to be **R**elevant to measure (and thereby to manage)

and it must be **T**ime phased, which means the value or outcomes are shown for a predefined and relevant period

In the earlier example of a KPI - to increase the average spend per customer from $50.00 to $60.00 (i.e. by 20%) by the end of June the following year - can you see how the KPI meets all of the 'SMART' criteria above?

"If you work just for money, you'll never make it. But if you love what you are doing, and always put the customer first, success will be yours."

<u>Ray Kroc</u> – McDonald's fast food restaurant entrepreneur

3. PRODUCT KNOWLEDGE

"The point to remember about selling things is that, as well as creating atmosphere and excitement around your products, you've got to know what you're selling."

Stuart Wilde – Self-help author and lecturer

The Importance of Product Knowledge

This chapter looks at why product knowledge is so important and how it forms an integral part of your role. As a salesperson, it is not only imperative that you understand the principles of what makes great customer service and how to perform sales; you must have good product knowledge about what you are selling in order to be successful. Good product knowledge is essential to demonstrate to your customer that you know what you are talking about. Having good product knowledge will enable you to confidently describe a product or service's features and benefits, and allow you to successfully answer any questions that your customer may ask during your conversation with them.

There is Always Something to Learn

No matter what type of product or service you are selling, there will always be things that you will need to learn about it. Knowledge specific to your industry may be learned from conventional methods such as induction training when you first begin in your role, but you may also need to seek out information yourself or ask management for their input on the industry you are in to give you a better understanding about what you are selling.

If you sell fashion items, for example, to have good product knowledge, you will need to know things like:

- what type of fabric or material an item is made from
- what other sizes and colours it comes in
- the best way to clean or care for the item
- whether or not there are coordinating pieces to go with it
- what accessories you could match with this item
- what type of occasions this item would be suitable for etc

If you work with food, you should be aware of things such as:

- what types of ingredients go into each item or dish
- how it is cooked
- how large the servings are
- what else is served with the dish
- whether it is spicy or not
- what other dishes would complement this dish
- whether it is suitable for vegetarians etc

These are all things that a customer could ask you in your role as a sales person, and it is in your best interest to have the correct knowledge to be able to assist them and increase your sales capacity.

Selling services also requires good product knowledge. If you are selling a service, for example, you would need to be able to answer questions from a customer such as:

- whether it is charged hourly or if there is a flat rate
- exactly what tasks the service entails
- what days of the week the service is offered
- if the service is also available on weekends, is a surcharge applicable
- how many workers will be doing the job etc
- are there any extra services that can be added on

The more you learn, the more you will want to learn. It will make your job more enjoyable, lead to increased sales and better career prospects!

Coming to Grips with Your Knowledge

Initially, if you are newly employed as a salesperson, or new to a particular department or area of your store, gaining product knowledge on everything that you are required to sell may take a little time. Induction programs for new employees usually always cover some product training, but often you will be required to seek out additional information you need on your own.

If, at any time, you feel that you don't have enough product knowledge to sell confidently, it is essential to ask your management to assist you in getting the training that you need. This benefits the business as well, as you will perform better in your sales roles once you are armed with better product knowledge.

Some companies offer e-learning, online training and regular in-store training sessions to help staff gain and maintain product knowledge. Management can often assist further by passing on the results of sales monitoring, company research, competitor analysis etc and general industry knowledge that comes with many years of experience. This will aid your sales process, giving you a greater understanding and fresh approach to how you sell things.

Don't always assume that you will be paid while you learn, however. Sometimes you will be required to undertake training on your own time. You should see this as a positive, not a negative, as any training or learning opportunities that you are given, only enrich your product knowledge and enhance your sales potential for the future.

Once you are familiar with the products or services that you sell and have a thorough grasp of product knowledge for your role, you will find that your job as a salesperson is easier. You will find it less difficult to build rapport with your customer and easier to gain their trust once they see that you can answer all their questions and provide them with the information that they need. Continuous self-improvement is essential, however, as initial product training may only cover the basics.

Maintaining Your Knowledge

It is important not to become too complacent with product knowledge, thinking that once you know how one product works, that anything similar will operate in exactly the same way. This may be true for some products – particularly things like computers or electrical products – however, you may find, for example, that certain models of a like product have very different features.

Maintaining your product knowledge on new items or services as they come into your store is crucial. This is particularly important if a product or service is being advertised and customer demand will be higher than usual. When demand is high, and trading is at a peak, with the right product knowledge, you will be well equipped to answer your customer's questions and win their trust for the sale. This is where having sound product knowledge will benefit you greatly over other team members who may not have as much.

Some companies will instill the services of a supplier or manufacturer to demonstrate new products to sales staff from time to time, to ensure that they are fully aware of any new features or functions that may differ from older models. This is a great way to gain expert product knowledge as you are usually handling the products, rather than just looking at a picture or packaging. You also have the opportunity to ask questions and clear up anything that you do not understand about the product.

Maintaining your knowledge on services your company may sell is also important, as conditions may vary for different or new services and it is vital that you convey the correct information to your customer.

Knowledge is Power

We have already touched on the fact that having good product knowledge builds self-confidence and enables you to confidently describe and sell a product to a customer.

Having good product knowledge, therefore, not only makes your job easier, but it empowers you as a salesperson. A customer who feels confident and comfortable with you as a salesperson because you are able to answer all their questions, is more likely to seek you out on a return visit to the store, than approach another team member whose knowledge may not be as good as yours. Repeat business (as we looked at in Chapter 2), can become a steady income stream, as it is much easier to sell to a repeat customer than it is to sell to a new one. Repeat business by regular customers will lead to increased sales.

Having good product knowledge also demonstrates to your manager that you are interested in what you sell and take your role seriously. This is a powerful asset in your favour at promotion time.

Understanding Sales Trends

Sales often tend to move in waves or patterns of similarity known as "sales trends". Generally, sales trends are referred to when sales of a particular product or service are increasing, 'though a steady or rapid decline of demand for a particular product or service is also a sales trend.

Studying sales trends helps retailers plan better for future sales, by either stocking up on popular items and reducing stock levels of unpopular ones, or reoffering a popular service and withholding those that did not sell so well.

When sales trends carry over from one season to the next, it is a lot easier to prepare stock levels in advance for the coming season, assuming then that the desired sales results will be achieved. If sales trends change suddenly and sharply, however, a retailer who has stocked up on a previously good selling item may sadly find that it is no longer as sought after and that sales may not be as high as expected.

As a salesperson, it is your responsibility to give adequate feedback to management on what items are selling best, what customers are asking for, what their complaints or issues might be etc. Management needs your help with this feedback to assist with their planning for current and future seasons. That last thing that you would want as a salesperson is to have is the wrong type of stock on the floor which is not popular and that you can't seem to sell. This will have a dramatic impact on your sales.

You should be aware of what the current sales trends are for the types of products and services that you sell, and where those trends are expected to go – that is, either increasing or declining. Matching products and with industry knowledge on sales trends will give you the best possible outcome in terms of sales.

For example, knowing what types of products sell best in particular seasons (for example, specific products that sell best at Christmas time or Mother's Day) will help you to make suggestions for customers who ask your advice on what to buy.

Similarly, being familiar with sales trends on a decline may, at times, deter you from selling a particular product to a customer, and instead, steer them in a different direction to a product that you know is becoming more popular and that in the long run, they will be happier with.

Knowing What's Hot & What's Not

As we have discussed, as a salesperson, it is advantageous to keep abreast of current sales trends to establish what is popular and not so popular in your particular field. Analysing sales reports can help determine the top selling and the lowest selling items, but will not always ascertain particular sales trends for coming seasons or where new products and services are concerned.

Following reports from overseas markets, industry journals and manufacturer's publications can all help to pinpoint trends for a particular product or service that may be relevant to your position. Knowing what is popular (or conversely, becoming unpopular) ahead of time is always an advantage in sales.

It is good to do your own homework and research on what is currently 'hot' (or not) in the marketplace, and to convey your findings to management. Be prepared, however, that there may be times that you will find that the 'hot' items which are actually selling the best, may not always be what you think they are..……..

Personal Preferences

Everyone is different in their personality and makeup, and personal preferences for one type of product over another will also differ. Different cultures and diversities of people, and different demographics will show different preferences for a range of products and services. Sometimes, a chain store in one suburb will sell significantly more or significantly less of a particular item over the same selling period than its sister store in another suburb. This is purely due to the different preferences of the customers in those particular areas.

Like the customers, you too will have your own preferences when it comes to the products that you are selling. Some you will like, others, you will not. Sometimes you will find that what is popular or what your customers want and are buying is not always what you may like or choose yourself. It is vital in sales, however, that you do not ever show your personal distaste to a customer's choice of a product, if their taste happens to differ dramatically from yours. You should refrain from letting your personal preferences be known or influence what you are offering or selling to your customers.

As always, ensure that you use active listening skills to make sure that you are matching the right product to the customer's needs, not using your own preferences as a guide. We will look at active listening skills in more detail a bit later on.

Why good product knowledge is essential –

➢ **Good product knowledge** gives you ⟹

➢ **Increased self-confidence** helping you achieve ⟹

➢ **Better sales results** which give you ⟹

➢ **More enjoyment in the workplace** and leads to ⟹

➢ **Better acceptance by co-workers & management** giving you ⟹

➢ **Better chances of career advancement**

"Success is a ladder you cannot climb with your hands in your pockets."

American Proverb

4. STORE PRESENTATION

"Give the public everything you can give them, keep the place as clean as you can keep it; keep it friendly."

<u>Walt Disney</u> – Creator of Mickey Mouse and Disneyland

The Importance of Store Presentation

In this chapter, we will look at the principles behind presenting your store in a way that makes it easy for customers to move around, find things and make their purchase, and factors that encourage them to buy. Good store presentation is essential if you want to draw customers in, keep them there long enough to make a purchase, and hopefully return for repeat business. The way a store is presented is directly related to the 'experience' a customer has while in the store, just as customer service is. A badly set up or laid out store, will not encourage shoppers to stay long enough to buy or possibly return at any point in the future. It may even prevent some from entering in the first place.

The layout of all stores will differ, depending upon the type and the sort of persona they portray. For example, a 'bulk buy' or 'discount' store may keep presentation very simple, just stacking boxes or pallets straight on the shop floor. Similarly, antique or bric-a-brac stores may deliberately present their stock in a jumbled or haphazard way, as customers in these stores find that fossicking for bits'n'pieces is half the fun. Other stores may strictly maintain a very neat and orderly appearance.

Often, using your own experience as a customer is a good guideline. If you walk into a store and see something that is both fantastic and really eye-catching or something that presents really badly, use that to benchmark how your own store is presented. Give feedback back on what you have seen to management. Fresh eyes can sometimes see things that get overlooked on a daily basis. It's not about being critical, it's about presenting a different point of view, and working with management on this will only better the business in the long run.

Things that you could 'checklist' to ensure good store presentation could include:

- Ensuring prices or barcodes are present on all goods
- Making sure shelf labelling and pricing is accurate for the goods that are displayed on them
- Ensuring that displays are clean, standing upright and looking symmetrically correct
- Making sure that trolleys or shopping baskets are accessible and plentiful
- Checking that brochures or catalogues are in the correct stands and are refilled regularly
- Ensuring that the correct music being played and if it is too loud or too quiet
- Ensuring that the overall ambience of the store is correct for its persona
- Ensuring window displays look dynamic and eye catching and are dust free

- Making sure that branding is visible
- Checking that walking paths are clear of obstacles and boxes and floors are clean
- Ensuring mannequins are suitably dressed and interacting with each other appropriately
- If an online business, checking for any obvious errors on your website, and ensuring that goods are being represented correctly in alignment with your branding and sales trends

Entrances & Exits

Entrances and exits in a store should be easy to see and easy to use. Depending on the type of store and the layout, the entrance and exit may be one and the same, adjoining, near each other, opposite each other or totally separate. Most are located near or in clear view of the counter/point of sale area, and some exits may only be by way of the checkout, for security reasons.

Whatever the set-up of the entrance and exit of your store, the principles relating to their purpose and how they function are essentially the same. The entrance should be clearly visible from the street front or mall entrance, be inviting and should draw people into the store. The exit should likewise be easy to find from within the store, easy to use, and essentially be via the counter/point of sale area or through a checkout, for maintaining store security. Wherever possible, the door to the store should be kept open to encourage spontaneous shoppers.

Point of Sale Area

The point of sale (POS) area is the counter, desk or checkout where the customer takes their goods to pay for them. This will generally house a POS system or cash register and facilities for processing EFTPOS and credit cards. Sometimes a point of sale area will be permanently staffed – like in a department store, or a checkout in a supermarket – and sometimes a staff member will simply accompany the customer to the counter or sales desk when they are ready to pay, like in a smaller boutique.

The point of sale area should be clean and uncluttered and provide an easily accessible surface for the customer to place their goods on while they are being attended to. This is particularly important in the case of a store selling clothing or fragile and delicate items. The point of sale area should always be well-stocked at all times with all necessary items such as:

docket/register/EFTPOS rolls
pens
tissue paper
carry bags
sticky tape
scissors
staplers
string
spare price tags etc
lay-by books or customer order books
gift voucher stationery etc

There is nothing more annoying for a customer than wanting to make a purchase by credit card and the sales assistant having to search high and low or worse still, leave the counter momentarily, to find a pen for them to sign with! Maintaining a well-stocked point of sale area will aid the speed of the sale and make the experience better for the customer. It is a good idea at the start of each shift to check that the point of sale area is well-stocked with all the essential items that you might need, particularly for peak traffic periods. (POS is covered in more detail in Chapter 18).

Signage

Signage throughout your store should be clear and easy for the customer to read and follow. Key areas of the store should be signposted for shoppers to follow. For example, if a customer has come to collect some goods that were placed on hold, they may have been told to collect these goods from the 'lay-by department'. If this department is located at the back of the store and is difficult to find because there isn't any clear signage, the customer is likely to become annoyed or agitated at the very onset of their shopping experience. Some customers may even walk out angrily and not proceed at all with collecting their goods or purchasing them.

Signage for areas such as the checkout or point of sale area, lay-by, enquiries, returns, escalators, lifts, toilets etc should be very visible for the customer and make it easy for them to find exactly what they need. Shelf signage too, should display clear messages with the correct shelf tickets displayed under the corresponding items. Ad banners and signage for sales and special offers etc should be clear and correct and not give misleading messages to customers.

In your role, you may not be responsible for things like the signage, but it is important to know and be aware of how signage is an important factor in the overall appearance and operation of the store.

Product Display

Just as the overall presentation of the store is important in creating a good impression on the customer, the way the actual goods or individual items on sale are displayed and presented is also crucial. Depending on your industry and your particular company, there may be specific rules in place relating to product display or 'visual merchandising' as it is referred to. Apart from obvious differences in how different types of product are displayed – for example, whether they are on shelves, hanging on racks, on display tables or stacked in piles on the floor – different companies often have their own preferences in how their products are displayed for sale. Product display may depend on the 'use by dates' of products, for example, if you are working in a retail environment selling food items.

Usually, specially trained staff known as 'visual merchandisers' will be responsible for the initial set up of product displays and deciding on how certain goods will be presented in the store. As a salesperson, however, it is in your best interest to ensure that those displays are maintained adequately, as this encourages sales. Imagine a clothing store where, after a busy lunchtime trade, half the garments were falling off the hangers, were turned inside out and crumpled on the floor. This would not encourage new customers who had entered the store later in the day to want to look at the clothes, let alone, try them on. This, in turn, would not encourage them to buy.

So, although it may not be your role to set up product displays in your store, it is your responsibility to keep the product looking its best and making it most attractive to the customers. This could mean things like:

- ensuring that all product is facing the same way
- making sure that where applicable, all product on a shelf is grouped into like styles and has the labels facing out so that customers can easily find and identify what they are after
- keeping products clean and dust free so they look more appealing – especially china or glass items
- making sure that items like shoes are paired correctly before putting them away in their boxes
- resealing boxes or items in packages that may have been opened by customers wanting to look at the contents

- making sure that change rooms are cleared quickly and ready for the next customer
- ensuring clothing is clean and crease free, with appropriate sizing and pricing attached

Quite often, you might find that your head office will supply photographic representations of how particular products should be displayed. This might be primarily for specific promotions of advertised lines or in seasonal periods such as Christmas. It is important that you are following the process set down by your head office. You may have your own ideas about how products could be displayed and these can of course be passed onto management, but not used in preference to those set out by the head office policies.

All these things are examples of how you can assist in maintaining product display to keep what you are selling looking fresh, attractive and appealing and consistent across the store, group of stores or website. This is what encourages customers to buy.

Music & Lighting

Industry studies have shown that both music and lighting in retail environments are significant contributing factors which encourage customers to buy. Just as you might use music or lighting to create a particular mood or atmosphere in your home, the same techniques can be used in a retail environment. It is proven that shoppers in a good mood, feeling relaxed and happy, will generally spend more in a single shopping expedition than those who are not feeling so jovial. Music, particularly, is often used to 'get shoppers in the mood for shopping'. Have you even wondered why nearly all retailers play Christmas carols throughout the stores in the weeks leading up to Christmas???

Music played in stores should be appropriate for the type of store and for the general demographics of the sort of customer it attracts, and should be played at a suitable level. Pop music, for example, is played in boutiques for the younger market - and often quite loudly - whereas more sedate music played at a softer level is usually found in a department store or boutique appealing to a slightly older age bracket. Again, there may be rules set out by particular companies as to the exact music that can be played in a store, but the reasoning for the music is the same. The whole idea behind the music is to make the shopper feel relaxed and in a comfortable environment that they can relate to. This can encourage them to spend more time in the store and possibly make more purchases.

The lighting used in a store should be bright enough to show the products off clearly, without being so harsh as to be unpleasant for the shopper. Different types of stores will use different types of lighting to create different moods and effects. You may have noticed when you have been out shopping yourself that a store selling candles and aromatherapy items, for example, will have much softer and subdued lighting compared to a store selling white goods. Can you think why??

Seemingly little things like making a regular check in your store to see that all the light bulbs are working – particularly in change rooms – can make a difference, too. A light being out is particularly frustrating for customers trying to match colours or see items clearly. Maintaining a good environment for your customers only adds to the good experience that you are trying to create for them, in order to hopefully make purchases.

Store Hygiene

In addition to keeping product in the store tidy and dust free, maintaining window displays and attending to the appearance of the store in general, store hygiene is an important factor that should be attended to, but is often overlooked. Regular checks should be conducted to maintain areas such as:

> counter tops
> door handles
> EFTPOS machines
> barcode scanners
> telephones
> change rooms
> staff meal areas and tearooms
> bathrooms
> as well as any back offices or meeting rooms

Regular maintenance of these areas will not only add to the overall appearance of the store - making it more appealing to customers – it will help to limit the spread of germs in the store, which can cause illnesses amongst the staff. Food outlets will have their own stringent guidelines relating to hygiene for both the kitchens and areas where food is served which should be adhered to at all times.

Before Opening

As a team, it is good practice to check over the store before the doors open to ensure it is clean, tidy, well-stocked and presented in an inviting manner, ready for trade. Most retail stores have an opening procedure with a checklist to ensure all aspects of the store are covered, in addition to a specific cash handling procedure for setting up tills or registers. It is important that the store presents well at all times, to make customers to feel comfortable whilst shopping and to encourage them to buy. As trade often increases through the day, if the store is not tidy and well-presented at the start, you might find that you end up getting into more and more of a mess as the day progresses, which is difficult to recover from and not good for business.

Shift Turnover

If you are ending your shift before the store is actually

closing, it is a good idea to do a quick check over the store before you leave, to ensure it is clean and tidy ready for the next team. If you have a specific section that you are responsible for, this should also be attended to. Doing this to assist team members is a common courtesy. No one likes to begin their shift in an untidy store. At peak trading times such as Christmas, when the store is busier than usual, untidiness may be unavoidable, but when it can be addressed, it is highly suggested to do so.

Closing

Similar to an opening procedure, most retail stores will also have a closing procedure to follow at the end of a trading period. Various aspects of the store will need to be attended to such as window displays, change rooms, counters, holds areas etc to ensure that they are clean and tidy ready for the next day's trade, as well as a cash handling procedure to balance tills and registers. It is important that the closing procedure is followed correctly to eliminate any tasks carrying over into the next day or for the next team. Sometimes, as part of the closing procedure, a shift report is to be written or filled in. This is a short account of the day's trade, including a note of any unusual or out of the ordinary circumstances, and it is used for the next shift or team, to read, understand to build on. It is also used at head office level, for them to get an understanding of any problems or issues that may be occurring in the store that they are not aware of, as well as an overview of the day's trade.

A typical shift report may include a variety of topics and questions and could even be in an online format for you to complete. If a shift report is part of the closing procedure at your store, ensure that you always complete it accurately and on time.

Following is a sample of the types of questions and answers that you might find in a typical shift report:

Date & day of the week	*Monday, 16th April 09*
Names of staff on duty	*Hannah, Josie, Isabella*
Weather conditions (i.e. extremely hot/cold)	*Nice sunny day*
Total number of sales achieved	*82*
Number of lay-bys (taken out & collected)	*3 taken, 1 collected*
Number of returns (include general details)	*2: 1 change of mind, 1 faulty zipper*
Number of gift vouchers sold	*1*
Top 5 selling items	*New logo t shirts, red scarves, black belts with big buckle, white hats, necklaces*
Was sales target reached today?	*Yes*
If no, why not?	*-*
If yes, what do you think helped contribute to this?	*New stock in window displays, t shirt promotion*
What is needed to help you sell more?	*Keep new stock coming in, more promotions*
Complaints received today	*None*
Commendations received today	*2 customers commented on the window displays*
Any unusual incidents	*No*

"Real integrity is doing the right thing, knowing that nobody's going to know whether you did it or not."

Oprah Winfrey – Business woman and talk show host in the USA

5. PERSONAL PRESENTATION & HYGIENE

"People are definitely a company's greatest asset. It doesn't make any difference whether the product is cars or cosmetics. A company is only

as good as the people it keeps."

Mary Kay Ash – Business woman and founder of Mary Kay Cosmetics

Personal Hygiene

Just as we have seen in Chapter 4, that store presentation and hygiene is important in a retail environment, personal hygiene is also vitally important in day to day life. If you remain clean and hygienic, your health will benefit. The opposite is true of the reverse.

In a sales environment, personal hygiene is an important factor, as you are representing your business when you are in front of your customers. Before every shift you should ensure that you shower, brush your teeth, are well-groomed with neat, clean hair and wear deodorant. This will assist you in being presentable to your customers and a good representation of your company. Your team members will also feel more comfortable if they are working with someone who is clean and smells nice.

It is also important to ensure that you wash your hands after going to the toilet. This will help prevent the transfer of bacteria and disease to your customers and your team members. If working in a food related field, this is particularly important. Specific rules apply to maintaining a clean and disease free environment when working with food and should be adhered to at all times. Normally, these are part of your induction or training and a checklist of such rules is often displayed in your work area.

Assisting with personal hygiene can sometimes be aided by the company that you work for. Some companies take this on as part of their responsibility by providing showers at the workplace for employees, and even deodorants for staff to use etc, but we recommend that you make it your responsibility to ensure that you are always well-groomed and well-presented during your shift.

A "personal hygiene kit" to carry with you or keep at your workplace is a good way to maintain good personal hygiene and remain well-groomed. Also arriving to work about 15 minutes earlier than required, to relax, cool down and stabilise the body back to its normal temperature is a good idea. This is particularly helpful if you walk or cycle to work, where you may not arrive as fresh as when you left home. There may be times throughout the day, too, where you may need to take 5 minutes to refresh yourself and reapply deodorant after unloading a delivery or stacking boxes, before you step back out onto the selling floor and liaise with customers. Smokers should be particularly careful to ensure that they use mints or mouthwash after a cigarette break to ensure that they return to the store with clean smelling breath.

Grooming

To ensure that you are presenting yourself well, you must keep your hair neat and (for men) be clean shaven. If you have long and messy hair, you may be presenting yourself as unprofessional. If you have facial hair, you must maintain it to ensure that it is neat and tidy. In some food environments, facial hair is unacceptable for health reasons. Consult your manager if you are unsure of the rules about facial hair within your business.

Fingernails, too, are a very important part of grooming. As a salesperson, it is important that you often handle or demonstrate a product in front of a customer. You want this product to look as appealing as possible to the customer. This will often not be the case if you are doing so with dirty and unkempt fingernails.

Again, working in food environments requires additional attention to areas of grooming like hair, fingernails, feet, cuts and sores etc. Hair should not only be clean, it should be tied back if long, or worn in a hairnet to prevent hair contaminating the food. Fingernails should be kept short and always meticulously clean when working with food. Even though gloves are used, dirty hands and nails are not appropriate in food environments for obvious health reasons. Similarly, open shoes are usually not permitted to be worn when working with food, for safety reasons and also for the health risk factors they pose. Any cuts or sores that you may have should have adequate clean and sterile dressings applied to prevent any chance of cross-contamination when working in a food environment.

Working with fashion would require you to pay particular attention to your make up as well as your overall personal grooming. Similarly, if working in the beauty industry, appropriate make up and impeccable personal hygiene would be particularly relevant.

Uniforms & Clothing

Personal presentation is of utmost importance when working in a sales environment. Your presentation will say a lot about you as a salesperson. Your uniform or clothing must be worn correctly and professionally. This means you must ensure that your clothes are washed and ironed prior to every shift that you work. If you do not have clean and ironed clothes, you will be presenting yourself as disorganised and unprofessional, and your customers may choose not to do business with you.

If your business requires you to wear a uniform, you must also ensure that you wear the complete uniform. This includes the appropriate footwear, pants, skirt or dress, belt, socks, hat, shirt or top and name tag. If your uniform is not complete, you may look out of place from your other team members and your business will appear to be disorganised.

If you are not provided with a uniform, you still must ensure that you are dressed professionally and suitably for your role. For example, a salesperson working in a high fashion boutique would be required to wear entirely different types of clothing to a salesperson working in a furniture showroom. Sales staff working in fashion outlets are generally required to wear the stock from the store to help promote it to the customers. In these cases, it is appropriate to wear clothing that might not be considered appropriate in many other retail environments. Working in fashion would also require you to pay particular attention to your shoes, to ensure that they are clean, in good condition and fashionable.

Generally, suitable attire in a sales role where a uniform or stock clothing is not provided would include :

FOR MEN –
Business shirt

Slacks/trousers
Leather dress shoes with dark coloured socks
Tie – in some instances
Jacket – in some instances

FOR LADIES -
Business-style shirt/top
Slacks/trousers
Skirt or dress of modest length
Suitable business-style shoes without excessively high heels

Usually, no denim, t shirts, sweatshirts, shorts, mini-skirts/dresses, overly high-heeled shoes, beanies, caps, low-cut tops or outfits showing too much skin are considered appropriate. Sleeveless tops or open shoes may also not be permitted if working in a food environment. It is very important to comply with company policy on any specific dress codes or regulations relating to clothing that may be in place with your company.

Jewellery, Piercings & Tattoos

As a general rule, keeping jewellery to a minimum during your shift is the best course of action, unless it's appropriate for your role. Sales staff working in the jewellery trade would obviously be required to wear some jewellery to entice customers into buying. Similarly, sales staff working in fashion roles are generally encouraged to wear jewellery and accessories to compliment the outfits they are wearing to also entice customers into buying.

Usually, if working with machinery, no jewellery at all is permitted for safety reasons. Chains hanging around your neck can be dangerous in many retail environments as they can easily get caught on things, especially if you lean forward over a product or display. Too much jewellery can also look very unprofessional, and does not usually look appropriate when wearing a uniform.

In recent times, piercings have grown beyond just pierced earrings for women – which is widely accepted and has been for many years. Now men, too, often wear earrings, and both men and women can display piercings in all sorts of weird and wonderful places which are not as widely accepted in society. Eyebrow, lip, nose and any other facial piercings may appear to be unprofessional. When working in a food environment, these and even ear piercings may be deemed unacceptable, as they will pose an occupational health and safety hazard as well as a food safety hazard.

Similarly, tattoos are now a popular fashion statement that is not widely accepted in most work environments. As with jewellery and piercings, displaying tattoos when working can all depend on your business' code of ethics or the type of industry you are in. As a salesperson, if you have piercings or tattoos, you need to be aware of whether or not it is accepted in your workplace and take the appropriate steps to conceal or remove them if not. Wearing appropriate clothing to hide tattoos or simply removing a piercing from your nose or brow during your shift is sensible if they are not deemed as acceptable for your role.

Mental Preparation

In addition to store preparation and preparing yourself physically for your day at work, mental preparation is a very important task that should be carried out before each shift. Arriving to work for your shift, not just on time, but early, so that you are not flustered or running late, will give you time to do a final uniform and personal hygiene check and carry out your mental preparation. Mental preparation before you start work is essential, to clear your mind of distractions and 'tune it in' to the day ahead.

There are many to benefits mental preparation. By taking just a few minutes to prepare yourself mentally before you start work, you will find yourself:

- in a calmer mood
- in a more organised frame of mind
- more productive throughout the day
- more 'in tune' with your customers
- more aligned with your team mates
- more capable of dealing with obstacles that present themselves
- and overall, more successful in reaching your sales goals

Mental preparation is easy to do and will only require 5 – 10 minutes of your own time. The best way to do your mental preparation is to sit quietly for a few minutes and think about things like:

- clearing your head of any personal issues that may distract you throughout the day
- dealing with any personal phone calls or text messages before you start work, then turning off your personal phone
- thinking about what's likely to happen in your day ahead
- thinking about whether there is anything special about today's shift
- thinking about what you need to achieve throughout the day
- thinking about team members - who you are working with today
- thinking if there was anything you were doing as a follow up from your last shift
- thinking about what do you need to provide your customers with today
- having a positive attitude to your day, your customers and your sales goals

At first, this might seem like a lot to do, but practicing every day, you will get better at it, and it will become almost an automatic action to get you into a work mindset, ready for your day. All this leads to better performance which leads to rewards for both you and the company. Always ensure, too, that you are up to date with any company communication like notes, memos, reports or notices that may have been sent from management, head office, other stores or the warehouse since your last shift.

Now you are ready for work!

Suggested items for your **personal hygiene kit** include:

> - deodorant
> - toothbrush & toothpaste
> - mouthwash or spray
> - breath mints,
> - hairbrush & comb
> - hair tie (if applicable)
> - nail clippers & file
> - nail brush
> - small mirror
> - hand sanitiser liquids or gels

This is a great way to maintain your personal hygiene and ensure that you smell clean and fresh during your shift.

"You don't get paid for the hour. You get paid for the value you bring to the hour."

Jim Rohn – American entrepreneur, author and motivational speaker

6. BEHAVIOUR & BODY LANGUAGE

"The golden opportunity you are seeking is in yourself. It is not in your environment; it is not in luck or chance, or the help of others; it is in yourself alone."

Orison Swett Marden - American author and founder of 'Success' magazine.

Understanding Behaviour & Body Language

Your behaviour and body language are important aspects of your personality that can convey certain messages to a customer, without using words. The messages they convey can be very powerful and can sometimes come across as negative and bad rather than positive and good. You are responsible for both your behaviour and your body language and you should be aware of them both at all times in your role as a salesperson.

Behaviour and body language are inter-related, in a 'cause and effect' kind of way - your behaviour tends to dictate your active body language, and your body language often reflects your next behavioral pattern. For example, if you stand with crossed arms while speaking to your customer, it will not send out positive messages, and will more than likely entice you to use more negative statements. Conversely, standing relaxed, smiling and using eye contact will bring on a more conversational connection with your customer and make them feel at ease.

General Behaviour

Behaviour is how you perform or act and the way you conduct yourself while performing certain tasks or actions. Your behaviour in relation to your role as a salesperson is very important, and starts from the moment you arrive at work to the moment that you leave.

During your shift, you are an active employee and a representative of the company. Your actions and behaviour will reflect on the company as well as you personally. Even while you are off the selling floor, or on a break away from the store altogether, you are still representing the company that you work for and your behaviour is important. You will be judged on your behaviour by people around you and there could be serious repercussions if you are not behaving well. This is particularly relevant if you wear a company uniform or an identifier such as a name badge with the company logo.

A good rule of thumb for behaviour is to use yourself as a benchmark. Always act in a way that represents how you would like to be treated by someone else. If you would not like to be ignored or made to feel unwelcome in a store, then don't treat your customers this way. Similarly, if you find that being assisted by someone who smiles and treats you courteously and with respect makes for a good experience as a customer, then give your customers that same type of treatment.

It is also important not to become blasé with your behaviour towards your customers. You may start your shift being very aware of your behaviour and actions, but slacken off later in the day, performing less efficiently. Remember, when customers arrive in the store, they are seeing you and experiencing your behaviour for the first time, regardless of how late in the day it is. It is no good only displaying good behaviour to those customers who arrive in the earlier part of your shift. All customers deserve good behaviour from you, always.

Unacceptable Behaviour

Unacceptable behaviour can have serious effects on your sales performance, and indeed have far more reaching effects on your role as a salesperson and possibly even your career. Undesirable behaviour towards a customer not only makes them less inclined to buy, it can shut down the channels of communication with them, make you appear unprofessional, untrustworthy and uncaring, and may even cause them to leave the store altogether.

Unacceptable behaviour can be as simple as ignoring customers entering and failing to greet them; leaning on the counter chatting, laughing etc with team mates; or continuing to talk on the phone when you can clearly see that a customer requires your attention. You should be constantly looking for new customers entering the store, acknowledging them, greeting them, and doing your best to assist them. Extremely unacceptable behaviour can lead to dismissal and even ruin your career.

Being unable to separate personal problems from work, and allowing these to impede on your performance can lead to negative or undesirable behaviour. Everyone can identify with "having a bad day" occasionally, however, you should not let this interfere with or dictate how you behave. You must be professional at all times and use ways to overcome personal issues, not letting them flow through to the customer.

A customer is there for a purpose, to seek out and hopefully purchase goods or services and you are there to help them achieve this. This is your professional duty. It is not appropriate to air your personal issues with a customer, or use this to work against your customers. For example, overcoming objections that a customer may raise, might be harder to deal with if you're already "having a bad day", but you need to work through this regardless, and remember your role, your sales goals etc. It is not the customer's fault that you are struggling through your day and it is vital that they should never be made to feel as though it is.

Being Judgmental

In your role as a salesperson, it is also essential that you are not judgmental in any way, and that you treat all customers and potential customers equally. Customers should not be judged in any form by race, colour, religion, sex, age, language skills, the way they dress, whether they are regular or non-regular customers, whether local shoppers or tourists, their social status, whether they are a celebrity or not etc. Everybody's dollar is important when it comes to sales and sometimes, you may be surprised at who has the most dollars to spend.

For example, to assume that a customer dressed very casually is less likely to be able to afford or want to spend money on goods or services than a customer dressed impeccably well in expensive looking clothing, would be a grave mistake as a salesperson. There are plenty of examples of casually dressed, unassuming customers who turn out to be very wealthy individuals with loads of money to spend. Don't make assumptions only based only on what you see. Remember, you should never judge a book by its cover!

Body Language

Body language is very important when it comes to selling. Body language is non-verbal and is the common term given to poses, gestures, facial expressions, hand & eye movements, which are usually performed subconsciously. Your body language will show the customer a lot about who you are and what your attitude is. Your customer will see more than they hear. You could be saying all of the right words but if your body language shows that you have a negative or greedy attitude, you are not likely to secure the sale.

Body language is often classified as either 'open body language' or 'closed body language'. Using open body language will help to put your customer at ease and assist in securing your sales. Open body language shows your customer that you are trustworthy and open to assist them with anything they need. You should look happy and ready to serve. Not only will this show your customer that they are welcome and that they can trust you, by moving towards your customers – generally in the midst of the store - it will also give you the opportunity to be aware of and greet any other customers entering.

If you display closed body language, however, you will not be showing your customer that you are willing or interested in helping them. Closed body language can display anger, upset or a general lack of interest. If you display closed body language, your customer is less likely to open up to you and give you all of the information you require to successfully make a sale. A customer is less likely to feel welcome in a store if the salesperson they see is displaying closed body language. More than likely the customer will feel very unwelcome in that store and leave without making a purchase.

Open Hand Gestures

Open hand gestures are important when selling. Using open hand gestures will help you to show your customer that you are trustworthy and welcoming. The more open you are with your gestures, the more likely you are to create excitement from your customer and a sense of trust in you as a salesperson. It can also come across to your customer as friendlier and less aggressive. For example, if a customer in a department store asked you where the nearest lift was, extending your arm with an open hand whilst explaining the direction that they need to go, rather than pointing with just your index finger and giving a short, sharp reply, is much more friendly to the customer and will make them feel much more at ease, putting them in a better frame of mind for purchasing.

When selling products, handling the product in front of your customer, opening the boxes or packages for them to see the item more clearly etc will show that you have passion and interest in what you are selling. This reinforces to the customer that you are genuine. This will also help to generate excitement in the customer about the product you are offering. If selling a service, spending time to give the customer as much background and helpful information as possible, perhaps giving them examples of previously satisfied customers who used that particular service, and assisting them with any questions that they may ask, will all help to generate interest and excitement in your customer in what you are offering.

While open hand gestures are very important, it is also important to ensure that your hand gestures do not take all of your customer's attention away from your conversation. Keep hand gestures to a meaningful limit for greater impact.

Greedy & Aggressive Body Language

Body language can also have the potential to make you look greedy or aggressive. If you are moving around briskly, rubbing your hands together or even talking very quickly, you will appear to your customer as though you are greedy for the sale and don't really have their best interest at heart.

It is of the utmost importance that you do not display to your customer that you could be thinking about how big your sale will be. You must always be showing your customer that you are doing what is right for them.

The more appropriate action as a salesperson would be to walk towards them, making eye contact, smiling, letting them know that you are happy to be of service. Stand neatly and comfortably without displaying any hint of hostility or bullying. It may be appropriate to put your hands by your side or behind your back.

Whilst eye contact is an important way of making your customer feel at ease, body contact with your customer, in most retail environments, is definitely not. This could be touching their arm or shoulder during conversation, or even trying to shake their hand when it is clearly not appropriate. Body contact will make your customer feel uncomfortable and pressured as you are invading their personal space. If you are using positive body language like smiling, eye contact etc, this will be sufficient and you will not need to use body contact in any form.

Reading a Customer's Body Language

Apart from being aware of your own body language, it is vital to learn to read the body language that your customer is displaying. If they are using closed body language, maybe you need to slow your sales process down and listen more to what the customer has to say or ask a few more questions. Don't launch straight into your sales pitch if you can see that it won't be well received.

Some examples of closed body language that a customer could display are:

lack of eye contact
arms crossed

edging away from you as you get closer to them
turning their back slightly or abruptly
rolling their eyes
displaying pursed lips or contorted facial expressions
leaning further away from you

Sometimes mimicking similar actions to what your customer is doing will help to make them feel more comfortable. Often this can be a slightly subconscious action as you are "getting in tune" with your customer and what they have to say. Mimicking must be done sensibly, of course. For example, don't scratch your nose or put your hand to your face every time they do, or it will have the opposite effect. Appropriate examples of mimicking would be leaning in a bit closer during a conversation if they do, changing to a more relaxed posed after a few minutes of chatting when they do or shifting your position slightly to face them more directly as they have done with you during your discussion.

Working in a Negative Culture

There will be times, that no matter how hard you are working in your role, you may find that unfortunately, there appears to be a negative culture or atmosphere at your workplace, and that everyone around you seems to have a very negative attitude about almost everything. It's difficult to feel and act positively in such an environment, and very easy to get caught up in that same negativity, displaying negative behaviour and body language, conveying negative messages. It is crucial, however, that you do not.

A negative culture is very detrimental. If you do find yourself in this situation, you need to rise above it. You need to be aware of your behaviour and body language, and what it conveys to the customer, at all times, remembering that your sales results and maybe your future career are based upon your behaviour and how you perform in your role. If your customers are receiving negative messages from you from your negative body language or undesirable behaviour or, they will not be encouraged to buy, and your sales will suffer.

Examples of open body language:

- smiling

- giving eye contact

- walking towards a customer

- facing your customer with your back to the wall

- using open hand gestures

Examples of closed body language:

- slouching over the counter

- standing with crossed arms

- having your back facing the centre of the store

- having pursed lips or contorted facial expression

Examples of greedy and aggressive body language:

- speaking very quickly

- rubbing your hands together while you speak

- moving around briskly

What to Do When "There is Nothing to Do"

Working in retail, you will come across many times when it is not busy. Assuming that if there are no customers in the store means that there is 'nothing to do' is not correct, and will display to your team members and management that you have a lazy or uncaring attitude towards your role. There are many things that you can use your time for when you are not busy serving customers. It is up to you to look around the store, and work out the best way to use the time that you have available.

If you have asked your manager about anything specific that they would prefer you to use this available time for, and still find yourself free, the following is a suggested checklist of things that you could do to maximise the time you have on your hands.

You could check things like:

Store presentation –
Is all visual merchandising correct?
Are there any boxes or obstacles on the floor?
Is there any general mess on the floor that needs tidying - packages that have been opened by customers etc?
Are any price tickets missing from items on display?
Do any items on the shelves need cleaning or dusting?
Do any clothing items need steaming or pressing?
Does the floor need vacuuming? (you must ensure that the store is totally free of customers if you are going to do anything noisy like this)
Are there any things in the store that need fixing? (you can make a list of these and contact the person that can help you)

Stock room –
Is there any stock here that can replenish shelves in the store?
Is there any rubbish lying around or boxes that can be removed?

Point of Sale area –
Does this area need to be restocked with docket rolls, pens, carry bags etc?
Are there any details from the previous sale that need to be completed?

Are there any updates or edits that can be made to the CRM (customer relationship management system)? *this may not always be done at POS

Is it appropriate to conduct or complete a random stock take of an area of the store?

Back office –

Does this need cleaning or tidying?

Do the cds/music need sorting?

Are there any customer mail outs to prepare or complete?

Phone –

Are there any calls that can be made to customers regarding lay-bys and non-payment of goods ?

Are there any non-urgent phone calls that need to be made?

Are there any appointments that need to be confirmed?

Are all previous phone messages followed up and thrown out?

Computer –

Is it an appropriate time to clean out the company 'inbox' of old messages?

Are there any updates or edits that can be made to the CRM (customer relationship management system)?

Are there any company social media requirement updates to be made online?

Head office –

Are there any daily, weekly or monthly reports to complete?

Is this an opportunity to contact head office for product knowledge assistance?

General –

Are there any competitors that need to be checked out locally or online?

Are there any customer complaints that need to be followed up?

Have you reviewed your own task list to ensure it is completed?

Is this an opportunity to spend some time learning from other team members?

Could you move an upcoming break time to now as it is quiet? (it could get busier again later)

Are you fully prepared for the rest of the day/week/month for anything special that may be coming up (for example, a product promotion)?

As you can see, there are lots and lots of worthwhile tasks that can be performed during times when the store is less busy with customers. Always make sure, however, that another team member can cover your position on the shop floor if you are carrying out tasks in the store room or back office, or if carrying out competitor analysis in neighbouring outlets. Never leave the floor unattended.

"It is your attitude not your aptitude that determines your altitude."

Zig Ziglar – Self-help author and religious speaker

Advantages of Keeping Busy

By utilising any 'down time' that you may have, you will achieve many things. Not only will this quiet period seem to pass by faster, you will be achieving things like:

- ➢ Keeping your store looking inviting and at its best, encouraging customers to buy

- ➢ Keeping your stockroom and back areas tidy and free of any unnecessary rubbish

- ➢ Keeping your POS area ready to serve customers and quickly

- ➢ Keeping your stock levels up in the store, which is far more important than available stock being stored in the store room

- ➢ Keeping your customer database and company social networking up to date

- ➢ Keeping up with phone messages, lay-bys and customer complaints

- ➢ Keeping up to date with any head office reporting requirements

- ➢ Utilising the time wisely to learn

- ➢ Showing your team members and management that you are a hard worker and that you are serious about your role

CARLO G SANTORO

7. WORKING TOGETHER

"Success seems to be connected with action. Successful people keep moving. They make mistakes, but they don't quit."

Conrad Hilton - American hotelier. Founder of the **Hilton** Hotels chain

Working in a Team

Generally, working in a retail outlet means that you will be working with other people, usually in a defined structure called a team. Just as the players on a sports team all work together to achieve a common goal, team members in a retail store all work together to help the store achieve its goals: to give great customer service and make sales. Whether a single store or multi-store company, all retail outlets will have a structure in place for their teams, with different members of staff holding different positions. We will look at these different positions shortly.

Multi-store chains are controlled by a head office, where most of the major decisions are made. The associated stores receive their instructions from the head office and all follow the same policies and procedures. Working in this type of structure means that the 'team' is not just made up of the people in your store, but those in head office and the other 'sister' stores that make up your group. Usually, you will have lots of contact with team members from head office and the other stores, 'though often 80% or more of the contact you will have with these other team members is by phone or email, due to the different departments, different locations in the city and suburbs, even different states. Whether the chain is 5 stores or 100 stores +, this will most often be the case.

An example of a basic 5 store chain and head office set up is displayed below. Your store might be part of a similar set up.

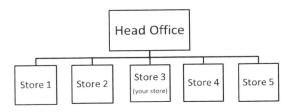

Team Structure

Inside your store, there may be many different types of staff. The usual combination is made up of:

Full-time staff - This may also include a store manager and a 'second in charge' (2IC).

(Some stores may also have a 'third in charge' (3IC) for times when the manager and 2IC are not available or are not rostered on)

Part-time staff - Generally not in managerial positions, 'though this is not always the case. (A 2IC or 3IC could be a part-time worker, for example)

Casual staff - Generally working a small number of hours per week in non-managerial roles

Understanding Hierarchy

If you work in a multi-store organisation, as your company gets bigger – i.e. more store locations across a larger geographical region - you will find more people in place in the team structure, as well as more workers collectively. Added to the basic mix of staff and team members that you would normally find in a single store as shown in the above table, a larger organisation which has many stores, would have additional team members in additional positions.

The order in which all these roles or positions fall is known as 'hierarchy' and refers to the level of responsibility or level of control or power that each position holds. The hierarchy in a company is usually displayed in a 'company structure' or 'oganisational chart'. Have a look at the following company structures to see how they differ slightly.

Single or smaller company store structure:

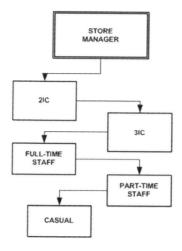

Larger, multi-store chain store structure:

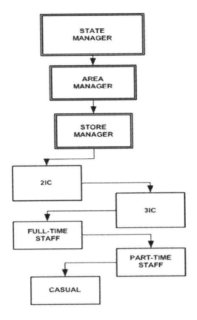

As with the team structure, the hierarchical structure or oganisational structure of a store may vary, depending on the size of the company and the number of people employed in the various roles. A store may or may not have both a 2IC and a 3IC; a store manager may manage more than one store and report to an area manager; there may or may not be an area manager as store managers may report directly back to the head office or state manager etc. It all depends on the company.

A 'duty manager' or 'shift manager' may also exist, responsible wholly and solely for organising till or checkout operators, staff break times, rosters etc for the duration of a particular shift - 'though this is usually more related with food outlets or supermarkets and department stores. A duty or shift manager may also cover for a store manager on certain shifts or days when the store manager is unavailable.

Examine the company structure that is in place where you work. It is important to know what each of the different levels of hierarchy represent and who holds each of those positions. Ask your manager if you are unsure about how your company structure is configured.

Working in a Structured Environment

One of the key factors in working in a structured environment is that when you start your shift, you are up to date and understand what has been going on prior. As we looked at in an earlier chapter, when preparing to start your shift, familiarising yourself and catching up with notes, memos, bulletins or staff update documents from managers or head office, to see if anything important is going on that you should know about, is a must. This not only makes your job easier as you will be up to date with any changes that may have taken place since your last shift, but it will show management that you are serious about your role and respect it. To make this easier, you may find that there will be a methodology in place to help team members – particularly casual and part-timers - keep up to date with what's been going on in the business.

Another key thing about working in a team environment and within different levels of management is to understand which team members in the various positions you should go to when you have a question, an issue to sort out, or a problem. Get to know the structure that may be in place in your store or company and ensure that you go to the right people. For example, you would normally refer all issues to your 2IC or store manager as opposed to going direct to someone in higher authority in the first instance.

Delegating

Part of working with a team means that quite often, in addition to your general duties as a salesperson, specific tasks may be allocated to you from management or a member of the team in a more senior role – a 2IC, for example - for you to complete during your shift. This allocation of tasks by a more senior staff member is known as 'delegating'. Delegating is a skill that is learned over time and is usually associated with the level of responsibility that you have, directly related to the position that you hold in the team. A casual staff member, for example, is highly unlikely to be delegating tasks to another staff member, but someone in a more senior role would regularly delegate tasks to other staff. As you progress in your role and become more senior with a higher level of responsibility, you will also be required to delegate tasks to other team members.

With the delegation or allocation of specific tasks to carry out, some will be able to be done in between serving – i.e. while you are not busy with a customer. But remember, the customer is always your first priority!

When you are allocated the task, ensure that you understand exactly what it is that you are expected to do. If you are not sure, make certain that you ask the team member who allocated the task to you, to explain it to you. There may be times, however, when that person may not be available. In these cases, you will need to use resources around you to assist you. For example, you might find that the information you need is stored on your computer system; you might call another store to ask them how to do it; or you may need to call head office for support. The main thing is that you endeavour to get the information you need to allow you to carry out and complete the task or tasks assigned to you.

When you have finished a task, it is also very important to ensure that you complete any associated paperwork or forms to show that it is now done or if not, why. Don't leave a task half-done unless there's a very viable reason. Perhaps you experienced some problems along the way and were unable to fully complete what was asked of you. Whatever the situation, this is important communication that shows someone else exactly where you are at or where you got to with the task and what has been done, keeping everyone is in the loop. A good flow of communication like this creates an harmonious team, with everyone working together successfully.

Most importantly, however, remember that the customer in front of you is always more important than answering the phone or carrying out any other tasks or jobs you may have on your list to do.

Break Etiquette

During the course of your shift, depending on the number of hours that you are working, you will be allocated certain times for breaks. Breaks are very important, and it is a legal requirement for you to have them. You need time to have a break from your job – both physically and mentally - and to refresh yourself with food and fluids. It is vital to plan breaks, working in with other team members to stagger each person's time off the floor, so that the store is not left with insufficient staff to serve customers. It is good etiquette too, to ensure (where possible) that you start your breaks on time and always finish on time so that another team member can then take theirs.

Be aware when you start your shift of what your allocated break times may be. This can be important as you can plan ahead to take care of any personal things that you may need to get done that day, around your breaks. For example, you may need to make phone calls about an appointment you may have later that day, or some plans that you have after work. You may even need to use your break time to attend a specific appointment.

Whatever the case may be, plan to do these types of things during your breaks, as you already have learned that you should not have your mobile phone on during work hours.

Use your break time for things like these:

Go for a walk to stretch and get some fresh air
Go to the gym – if time permits
Do your shopping
Make phone calls
Have some food, tea, coffee, water, cigarette etc
Attend appointments
Read a book or magazine
Run errands – pay bills, postage etc

Another important reason for taking your breaks is to allow you to eat, drink, smoke, make personal phone calls etc away from the shop floor. Under no circumstances should you eat or smoke near customers or merchandise. Even in a back room, the smell of food or cigarettes can travel into the store and is not a nice experience for customers. Also, when you are on your breaks, as we have touched on before, if you are wearing a uniform, be conscious that you are still representing the company whilst you are out, and you are identifiable. Sometimes it may even be preferable to cover the uniform or remove it while you are on a break.

The main aim of your break is to REFRESH, REFUEL & RELAX.

Personality Differences

Throughout your career, you will work with many different types of people, who display a variety of character traits, which make up their various personalities. People will display different moods; have different ways of expressing themselves; react to situations in different ways; and go about their day in entirely different ways to the way perhaps you or someone else would. No two people are exactly alike, but there are some common character traits or 'personality types' that you will come across. We've broken these common 'types' down into four distinct groups. Have a look at the chart at the end of this paragraph to examine the different groups that exist. See if you can work out which group you fall into………

On a daily basis you may work with some or all of these different types of personalities. Some you will find that you may connect and work with well and some, not so well. The main thing to remember is that these different personality types do exist and once you recognise the different types that exist in your workplace, you need to find ways to work well with all of them. For example, you might like to try and work out what personality types some of your co-workers have and use this information to try and find better ways to 'connect' with them or to understand what makes them tick!

Cultural Backgrounds

You could also work alongside a variety of people who come from many different economic and social backgrounds. These factors together with race and religion can sometimes influence how a person acts in certain situations. It is important to remember that not everyone thinks like you or has had the same experiences as you and therefore will not always act the way you do or the way you expect them to in a certain situation. The best way to all work together successfully is to ensure that you listen to your colleagues, understand and learn from them. Most importantly, everyone in the team should always be treated equally and respected for any cultural differences present.

Understanding Your Customer

Customers who come into your store all have needs. They might want a quick price check; need a replacement item for something that has stopped working; a bigger size; a different colour; a gift suggestion etc. They will also all have certain personality traits which will influence the way they express their needs or come across to you.

As a salesperson, it is your role to service their needs no matter which way they might come across. Treat them all as equals, as they are all potential customers. They might buy now, tomorrow, next week or tonight online. They could phone up later today or on the weekend, or walk into another one of your shops tomorrow to fulfill their needs. Your job is to make sure that no matter what type of personality trait or cultural background a customer has or displays, the service that you give is of the highest level and makes it easy for them to buy.

There may be times when you experience what you may feel is negative behaviour or a particular 'attitude' from a customer. It is important to remember, however, that a customer's attitude in the store may not be related to you. It may be related to an external factor. For example, they may have just been issued with a parking ticket, missed the train, or been up all night with a sick child. Or, they may be just having a 'bad day'. Whatever your customer's attitude may be, you want to try and make them feel at ease whilst in the store and you don't want to give them a reason to leave. Whether they are flustered or appear out of sorts, continue to offer outstanding customer service regardless, as, ideally, while they are in the store now, you want them to buy.

"There is only one boss - the customer. And he can fire everybody in the company from the chairman on down, simply by spending his money somewhere else."

Sam Walton - American retailer. Founder of Wal-Mart.

PERSONALITY TYPE	DESCRIPTION	CHARACTERISTIC TRAITS
Type 1	Strong leaders who tell people what to do & are completely responsible for anything that happens in the store; display excellent leadership skills; expect respect	responsible, committed, orderly, authoritive, loyal
Type 2	Persuasive people who use open & emotionally based language to get results; get on very well with people in general; very good communicators; most likely to sit down with you & discuss how to handle a problem or situation; get results but in a different way to the strong leader type	'people people', open, communicative, influential
Type 3	Someone who just works with the situation the way it is & gets on with things; doesn't question or push back; might have their own way of doing things, but just get on with the job	approachable, steady, consistent, reliable
Type 4	People that run by the rule book & seek perfection; follow lists & procedures; no swaying from the task at hand; difficult to influence; if a checklist says to do a particular task, they won't stop until the task is done	methodical, structured, thorough, perfectionists,

Many wonderful personality profile testing systems exist. For example, refer to Myer-Briggs or DISC Personality Profiling.

8. OCCUPATIONAL HEALTH & SAFETY

"It's easier to go down a hill than up it but the view is much better at the top."

Henry Ward Beecher - Clergyman, orator, editor and author

What is OH & S?

Occupational health and safety (OH & S) is literally a company's responsibility to ensure the health and safety of their staff while performing their duties in their particular occupation. OH & S regulations exist for all industries in all countries. Some industries – particularly those where operating equipment and machinery is involved – would have more complex rules in place than perhaps an office or a retail environment, but OH & S is vitally important in any type of workplace, and all companies must abide by the governing regulations in place for their country.

The enforcement of stringent OH & S laws is a great thing for the staff of any business as it ensures that while you are present for your designated work hours, that your safety is looked after and that you will be able to do your job and perform the tasks allocated to you without getting hurt or injured, or endangering your health in any way. The ruling ensures that you will not be asked to perform any duties that could put you in any danger, and it also enables you the right to ask for assistance from members of your team if you need help to perform a particular task, to ensure that you do not get hurt. Most companies will have a designated 'health and safety officer' or 'OH & S officer' – a particular member of the team who is responsible for maintaining and enforcing the health and safety guidelines within the company, and is the person to report any incidents or accidents to, to ensure that the correct action is taken. Often the health and safety officer will be identifiable by a yellow hat, 'though this is not always the case. Depending on the size of the company, there may also be more than one person in this position.

Working in retail, you will of course find OH & S guidelines in place. These may range from instructions on how to lift correctly, how to avoid common workplace hazards, and what you should do in the case where an accident does occur and you or someone in the team is injured.

To promote good OH & S practice, make it a priority to:

- familiarise yourself with all the OH & S rules in place in your company
- identify who your health and safety officer is
- ensure that you know how to contact them in an emergency

Common Sense

In any environment where safety is an issue, whether you are at work, home or out, you need to make sure that you are considering both your health and the health of the people around you, by using common sense. This may be in relation to how to pick something up, where to put something, how to perform a particular task using an instrument like scissors or a blade etc. Quite often, all that is needed to maintain a safe environment is to think carefully and display good common sense. For example, you would not try to move an extremely heavy box on your own. Common sense would tell you to ask for help and perhaps put it onto a trolley to make it easier to move around. Keeping yourself fit and healthy with a good diet, exercise and plenty of sleep also helps to maintain good general health and make you less likely to get sick.

Common Hazards in the Workplace

Believe it or not, working in retail, you will come across many different types of hazards or potential dangers, which you need to be aware of. Some of these hazards are not dangerous in themselves, but can lead to accidents or potential danger if they are not used correctly or common sense and regulation guidelines are not followed.

For example:

- Boxes left on the shop floor could lead to staff or customers tripping over on them.
- A ladder left out after hanging a 'sale' sign could lead to customers trying to use it to reach something on a top shelf and falling from the ladder.
- Empty stands or mannequins left out on the floor could lead to them falling on a customer and causing injury
- Cables and electrical cords could lead to staff or customers tripping over on them. This applies to cables on the shop floor and also cables behind the counter area where staff are moving around.
- Food or drink spills from customers entering the store could lead to the floor becoming slippery and customers or staff slipping over.
- Items being dropped and broken onto the floor could lead to staff or customers tripping or slipping over.

Serious injury could occur if the items broken contain glass or china.

Hazards like those listed above can be very common in a retail store, so it is important that you be aware and attentive at all times of the potential danger that they can cause. Returning equipment like ladders and cables back to where they came from, removing any boxes from the floor and attending to spills and breakages quickly can help ensure that no accidents or incidents will occur. With spills and breakages, the safest procedure to follow is to quickly mark the area where the spill has occurred with the appropriate signage or barrier to prevent customers walking in that spot and slipping over, then have the spill cleaned up as quickly as possible.

Preventing Hazards

The very best way to address hazards in the workplace is to try and prevent them to begin with. As we have seen above, this is done by keeping walkways and shop floors clear, removing ladders and boxes and cleaning up spills etc.

Part of your daily procedure for maintaining store presentation should include keeping an eye out for preventing potential hazards.

Safe Lifting Techniques

As a salesperson you may often be required to lift stock or boxes of stock and move it from place to place. Part of good OH & S is to always follow safe lifting techniques so that you do not hurt yourself. Safe lifting involves being aware of what you are about to lift and if you will need help from another team member, a stronger team member or perhaps a trolley. Unless you know exactly what it is that you are about to lift, it's good to do a quick test by tilting the box or item a little and putting your hand underneath it quickly to test the weight. You should never attempt to lift more than 20kgs on your own, so if you think that this could be the case, then you should call for another team member or a stronger team member to assist you. You might also use a trolley to help.

Safe lifting technique also involves getting close to the item and bending at the knees, using the power in your legs to get you upright and lift the box or object, without bending your back. Incorrect lifting procedures can be extremely harmful and in particular, cause severe back injury which be long-lasting and very debilitating.

Safe Storage

In a retail environment, stock will not only stored on shelves and racks within the store, but often, a stockroom or back room will house excess stock for replenishing what's sold, or stock that may be out of season or part of a past (or future) promotion that needs to be kept off the shop floor at a particular time.

Regardless of where the stock is located, it is an important OH & S factor to ensure that all shelves and racking are safe and that the correct storage devices are being used.

This means that the shelving or racking you are using is correctly suited to take the weight of the stock that it is holding, and that there is no danger of it buckling or collapsing because it is being used to house products that is wasn't designed for. You should also ensure that there are no loose screws or sharp edges on the racks and shelving that can catch on people's clothes or cause scratches as they walk past or reach in to get things out. Garments are normally hung on special racks and again, you should ensure that these are capable of bearing the right load and not in danger of collapsing.

Safe storage is particularly important for some items that are temperature sensitive like food items. You must always ensure that you are following the correct storage procedures for these items, storing them in the correct manner, at the correct temperature and for the recommended length of time only. It is usually mandatory that all food items are stored in airtight containers or bottles & jars to prevent spoiling.

Cross Contamination

A vital OH & S guideline to be followed – particularly if you are working in the food industry – is taking steps to prevent cross contamination of bacteria on food preparation or food serving areas. Strict rules on food preparation and food storage methods are usually in place in any retail outlet serving or preparing food and must be adhered to at all times to prevent the spread of germs which cause disease and serious illness.

If you have a designated lunch room or staff meal area in your store, you should also be aware of how to avoid cross contamination by keeping table tops and benches clean and disinfected, and being careful not to put food down on surfaces that may be unclean, such as tops of boxes, packages or benches used for packing or storage. Cleaning up after yourself will also help maintain a clean area for other team members to use.

Fire Extinguishers & Fire Exits

You may notice around your store or in selected locations such as a back office or under the counter that fire extinguishers are kept. These are vital, of course, if there is a fire in your store and it is good OH & S practice to be aware of the different types of extinguishers and how to use them if needed. Generally, there are two types of extinguishers that would be present in your store – one for paper/wood/general fires and one specifically for electrical fires. There is a big and important difference between the two, and all staff should be aware of this to ensure that in the case of a fire, the correct type of extinguisher is used. Using the incorrect type of extinguisher can not only be ineffective, but in some cases can cause life threatening situations.

Normally, part of your orientation as a new staff member would include basic training on the different types of fires that can occur and which extinguishers to use. You may never actually need to use one, but it is good practice to be aware of. Your manager or head office would generally ensure that all the extinguishers are kept in working order, with an external company normally responsible for the regular maintenance and any repairs required.

Your store, like any business, would also have an 'exit plan' in place in case of an emergency such as a fire, security or lockdown issue. The exit plan would entail ensuring that all customers and staff vacate the store in a quick and orderly manner, with staff assembling at a designated meeting point. This is to ensure that all staff present on the day are accounted for and that no one is left in the store. It is a requirement by law that all fire exits in the store are clearly visible and lead to a secure area outside the building.

There is normally a copy of your store's 'exit plan procedure' or 'fire safety procedure' displayed in the office or back room with the steps to be followed and a map showing the allocated meeting place after exiting. If you do find yourself having to evacuate the store for some reason, ensure that any team members that are working with you along with any customers in the store are evacuated quickly and safely.

Regardless of what type of retail environment you are working in, all OH & S issues are very important and should be considered and followed at all times. When you are going about your daily routine however, as a salesperson, as always, don't forget that the customer is the most important consideration of all!

Here are some more ways that you can help to **prevent hazards** in the store during a typical working day:

➢ Be aware of stock sitting on shelves that may be too close to edge and can be knocked by a passing customer or trolley, or caught on someone's handbag. Keep stock away from the edges.

➢ Keep liquids away from computers, scanners, EFTPOS machines and security devices

➢ Ensure that all the computers and electrical devices are plugged in correctly and that no cords are left hanging

➢ Take care with sharp implements when opening boxes

➢ Keep good ventilation around your computer box (which is often inside a cupboard or under the counter) by not putting anything on top of it. It needs air to keep cool, otherwise it can be a fire hazard

➢ Boxes delivered to the shop floor may need to be stacked out of the way of shop traffic until they can be unpacked

---

"The most important adage and the only adage is, the customer comes first, whatever the business, the customer comes first."

Kerry Stokes - Chairman of Seven Television Network, Australia

9. RETAIL FIGURES & FORMULAE

"It's a very tough market. So unless you do a really good job, you buy the right products from the manufacturers, you service the customer, they keep coming back, they bring their friends in, it's all about numbers, numbers, numbers."

John Ilhan - Founder of the Crazy John's chain of retail stores in Australia

Understanding Retail Formulae

Even though in your role as a salesperson you would not be responsible for determining pricing structures in your store, it is important to know what some of the commonly used terms for calculating and establishing costs and selling prices mean and how they relate to the business overall.

To keep operating and to enable them to grow and expand, all businesses need to make money. They need to generate more money from their sales than what it costs them to run the business, in order to get ahead.

The basic financial strategy of any retail business can be simplified as follows:

1.   Establish the minimum **gross profit** required to get above the '**break even**' point, by understanding *all* the **operating costs** and **COGS** (**cost of goods sold**) involved in running the business

2.   Understand and set the required **gross margin** to do this

3. Establish the **mark-up** required on products to achieve the **gross margin**

If all this is done correctly, the business will generally generate profit, which is, of course, the goal..

Commonly used retail formulae terminology:	
Profit	The difference between what the company's overall costs are compared with the money it takes in through its sales. It is the *outgoings* (costs) compared with the *income* (sales). The income needs to be higher than the outgoings in order for the store to make a profit. Profit can be defined in two slightly different ways: *gross profit* and *nett profit* * *Gross profit* = *sales minus COGS (cost of goods sold)* * *Nett profit* = *gross profit minus operating costs*
COGS	is the *cost of goods sold*. This means the price to purchase or manufacture the goods that are being sold, *plus* any associated costs to get the goods to the store —eg: freight or insurance charges
Operating costs	Also referred to as '*expenses*', these are additional costs that the business incurs as part of its day to day operation — eg: electricity, rent, wages, phones, advertising etc

Break-even point	The point where the outgoings are equal to the income, so the business is not losing money, but it is not making money either. This is better than making a loss, but a business needs to get past break even and make profit in order to survive and grow
Mark-up	The *amount added to the cost price* of an item to reach the selling price or retail price which the customer pays. This can be represented by a dollar value or a percentage. * *Mark-up = profit divided by cost*
Margin	The percentage amount of income required by a business to make it profitable. Margin can be defined in two slightly different ways: *gross margin* and *nett margin*, the calculations based on either *gross profit* or *nett profit* * *Gross margin = gross profit divided by sales* * *Nett margin = nett profit divided by sales*

Don't worry if you weren't sure exactly what some of those financial terms meant. We'll have a closer look now at a few of these and some of the other most commonly used terms that you will hear in relation to retail figures and formulae and establish what each of these terms mean.

Profit, Mark-up & Margin

Of all the terms defined above, *profit*, *mark-up* and *margin* are perhaps the terms that are most commonly referred to, and sometimes the most misunderstood. *Mark-up* and *margin*, in particular, are often interpreted as one and the same, which is incorrect. We will look at each of these terms in more detail, with some examples in figures, to help you understand exactly what each one means and how each one is calculated.

To do this, have a look at the following table representing the income earned and the outgoings payable for a pretend store: Sammy's Sports.

Sammy's Sports trading results for the last financial year:

	INCOME GENERATED	COSTS INCURED (OUTGOINGS)
Store sales	$500 K	
COGS		$250 K
Expenses		$100 K
Total	$500 K	$350 K

PROFIT

As we have already discussed, the term 'profit' refers to the difference between what the company's overall costs (outgoings) are compared with the money it takes in through its sales (income). Profit is perhaps the most important financial factor of all. For a business to continue operating, it needs to continually make a profit. Profit in a store is achieved by increasing the cost of products that it buys from a wholesaler or manufacturer (or what it may manufacture itself in the case of a food outlet, for example), to create a selling price, to sell the products to the customers. The selling price or 'retail price' of an item should always be higher than the cost price for a store to make a profit.

Profit is what pays for all the expenses within the company to keep it running – things like wages, rent, electricity and phone bills, marketing and advertising costs etc. Any further profit leftover greatly benefits the company, as it then has money to reinvest into the business to aid in future growth.

As a salesperson, it is your role to continue to make sales, which keeps the company making a profit. Things like damaged goods, theft and heavy discounts or continual price reductions all eat into the profit of a store, and affects the long term success of the business. This then can affect your future and the security of your job. This is a good thing to remember if you are ever tempted to offer discounts too freely, particularly to friends and relatives that may visit your store.

Gross Profit

In the previous example, Sammy's gross profit is calculated as:

> Gross profit = sales – COGS ➡ Gross profit = $500K - $250K ➡ Gross profit = $250K

Nett Profit

In the previous example, Sammy's nett profit is calculated as:

> Nett profit = gross profit – expenses ➡ Nett profit = $250K - $100K ➡ Nett profit = $150K

Can you see from these examples above how profit is easily recognised as income generated minus outgoings ?

MARK-UP

'Mark-up' is the amount that a product's cost price is increased by to give the end selling price or retail price. Mark-up is added onto the total cost the store incurs to purchase a product or service (COGS), in order to create a profit. This increase (the mark-up) can be referred to in a dollar amount or a percentage amount.

Not all products in a store will have the same mark-up. Some items will have a higher mark-up than others. Decisions on how much mark-up a product should have is at the discretion of the store owner or head office when they are setting the pricing structures for all the products sold. In your role, you would not normally be required to calculate mark-ups, but it is important that you understand how they work.

Gross Mark-up

As not all products in a store will have the same mark-up, the trading results for Sammy's Sports will give a very generalised example of how mark-up on an item is calculated:

> Gross mark-up = gross profit ÷ COGS x 100 (to give mark-up as a %) ━▶ Gross mark-up = $250K ÷ $250K x 100 ━▶ Gross mark-up = 1 x 100 ━▶ Gross mark-up = 100%

Looking at this calculation another way using Sammy's figures, if Sammy uses a 100% mark-up on the cost of his stock across the board and sells it all, he will be effectively doubling his money, making a gross profit of also 100% :

> COGS x gross mark-up = gross profit ━▶ $250K x 100% mark-up = gross profit ━▶ $250K x 100% = $500K

Can you see from these examples above how the calculations are achieved and how the elements that make up the calculations are inter-related?

Mark-up on an individual product

Next, we'll look at a further example of mark-up, but this time on an individual product (eg a bicycle), to again show how the calculations are made.

In this example, Sammy buys some bicycles from a wholesaler for $120.00 each; pays $10.00 per bicycle in freight costs to get them to his store; uses a 50% markup on the total cost of the goods purchased (equating to $65.00 in this case); to sell the bicycles to customers in the store for a retail price of $195.00.

COST OF GOODS FROM THE SUPPLIER	ASSOCIATED COSTS FOR THE ITEM	TOTAL COST FOR THE ITEM	MARK-UP	RETAIL PRICE (END SELLING PRICE TO CUSTOMER)
Bicycle bought from wholesaler for $120.00	Freight $10.00	Purchase price + freight cost	Amount added to the total cost for the item to give the retail price	$195.00
Total: $120.00	Total: $10.00	Total: $120.00 + $10.00 = $130.00	$130.00 + $65.00 (or 50%) = $195.00	Total: $195.00

MARGIN

'Margin' is the amount of income that a business needs to generate to cover all its costs and expenses, in order to make it profitable. As we have seen earlier, margin can be defined in two slightly different ways: *gross margin* and *nett margin*, the calculations based on either *gross profit* or *nett profit*.

Margin is often confused with mark-up, but whereas mark-up is calculated on costs, margin is calculated on sales.

Gross Margin

Referring back to the earlier 'trading results for the last financial year' for Sammy's Sports as our example, the gross margin that Sammy has achieved through his sales is calculated as follows:

Gross margin = gross profit ÷ sales x 100 (to give mark-up as a %) ━▶ Gross margin = $250K ÷ $500K x 100 ━▶ Gross margin = 0.5 x 100 ━▶ Gross margin = 50%

Nett Margin

Using the same calculation method as above, similarly, Sammy's nett margin is calculated as follows:

Nett margin = nett profit ÷ sales x 100 (to give mark-up as a %) ━▶ Nett margin = $150K ÷ $500K x 100 ━▶ Nett margin = 0.3 x 100 ━▶ Nett margin = 30%

If you've been able to follow all the calculations shown in these examples, you are well on your way to having a good understanding of the most commonly used formulae in retail. Don't worry, however, if you are not quite there yet. As a salesperson, you would not be expected to perform these calculations; it's just good to have an understanding of what they mean and how they are used.

The 3 most basic retail formulae that you might need to know in your role, however, are:

Cost of Goods + Markup = **Retail Price**
Retail Price - Cost of Goods = **Markup**
Retail Price - Markup = **Cost of Goods**

If you refer back to the example for the sale of the bicycle, it will help you to understand how all these formulae are inter-related. You might like to practice some calculations using these basic formulae to help you fully grasp the concept.

There are many more calculations that can be looked at and lots of formulae that can be explored, but we will look at some of these in future chapters. At this stage, however, the basic principles that you should remember in terms of retail figures and formulae are:

- ➢ A store must generate **profit** to stay in business
- ➢ **Profit** is created by **selling goods** at **retail prices**
- ➢ **Cost price** is **marked up** to create the **retail price**
- ➢ **Discounts** and **theft reduce profit**

Loss Leaders

You might sometimes hear the term 'loss leader' when working in retail. This term refers to an item or items that may be sold to the customer at or below their cost price, as opposed to having a mark-up applied. The use of loss leaders is particularly common for a new store as part of its opening advertising campaign. For example, a new clothing store might advertise t shirts for sale for $4.00 each when in fact, the cost price is almost $5.00 each. In this instance, the store is placing more emphasis on attracting customers to the store, rather than making money on the sales of the actual item being promoted.

By advertising products at or below cost, it encourages customers to come into the store who might otherwise not have visited. Once the store has brought customers in, it then has the potential to sell the customer other items which do have mark-up applied and will generate a profit for the business. Sometimes, especially for a new store opening, or a store that is going through a quiet time, it is harder to get customer traffic through the doors than it is to actually sell them something while they are there. This is why the use of loss leaders is a great marketing tool and works very well to generate new customers for a business who will presumably return and buy again in the future.

Here are some more reasons why a store might use a 'loss leader' such as the t shirt example above.

- Creates customer awareness of the store – particularly if it's new
- Gets lots of customers through the doors
- Gives potential for making further sales of profitable items once the customers see what else is for sale in the store
- Gives the customer a great bargain buy which they will be very pleased with

Volume Sales

'Volume sales' refers to the process where a store might package up multiples of the same item at a reduced price, to encourage sales and allow them to move larger numbers of or larger volumes of stock. Often these will be items that may have a low mark-up and provide less profit for the store, so a higher volume of these items needs to be sold in order to keep profit flowing.

For example, in a department store, a pair of men's socks might only generate around $1.00 profit per pair, compared with a business shirt that may generate $20.00 profit. The store would need to sell around 20 pairs of the socks to equal the profit made by the sale of one business shirt, yet the time and energy involved in selling the socks might be the same. If the store then packages up five pairs for the cost of three, more customers will be encouraged to buy the socks and higher volumes of the socks will be moved. In this instance, even though there will be a slight drop in the profit because of the discounted price, the store will still sell more socks in this way than at the original standard price per pair, and will benefit from the greater volume of sales. This is a common practice that you might see used in your store around 'sale' time, and is helpful in moving not only volumes of low profit items, but slow sellers and out of season items that may have become a little less popular because of the time of year. We will look at more detailed information on volume sales a bit later.

Sales Targets & Retail Formulae

As we looked at in an earlier chapter, in your role as a salesperson, you will have certain sales targets to achieve either per shift, per week, per month or even per quarter. These targets together with key performance indicators (KPIs) will have been set by management and calculated using a combination of some of the retail formulae we have been looking at here. Regular reviews will be made to these targets – week to week; month to month or even day to day - with modifications made where necessary to ensure that the business continues to operate profitably. Variations in sales, labour costs, changes in customer traffic etc can all affect profit margins and can at times lead to cuts in employees' hours or at worst, laying people off.

Relationship Building & Improving Your Margin

When you give great customer service and build relationships with your customers, you are constantly increasing the possibility of improving your sales and increasing your KPIs. The better service you give, the happier the customers will be, and the more likely that you will not only succeed in closing the sales, but will do so without having to offer discounts just to secure the sale. Some customers may be more reserved in a sense and indicate that they are just there to buy, not interested in making much conversation etc. They may have checked out competitors' prices and may push you for a discount or a better deal or they may just be in a hurry. You still need to continue to offer the best customer service that you can, however, as these customers still offer potential sales for you, not only today, but again as repeat customers in the future.

As a general rule, relationship building with your customers is always important as part of great customer service, and it can lead to increased benefits for you as a salesperson as well!

"The difference between the impossible and the possible lies in a person's determination."

<u>Tommy Lasorda</u> - Former Major League baseball pitcher & manager

* If you'd like to challenge yourself a little further on the concept of retail figures and formulae, see if you can fill in the missing figures in the following table. (The answers are at the back of the book!)

Cost price $	Selling price $	Profit $	Mark-up as % (profit/cost *100)	Margin on sales as % (profit/sales *100)
10	20			
35	70			
	30	10		
100	130			
100		150		
80			75%	
65			100%	
1,000	1,500			
1,000				50%
100,000		80,000		
2	20			
		100	100%	
		500	33%	

10. COMPETITOR ANALYSIS

"You've got to look for a gap, where competitors in a market have grown lazy and lost contact with the readers or the viewers."

Rupert Murdoch - Chairman of News Corporation

Understanding Competitor Analysis

Competitor analysis is an important part of your role as a salesperson. It is imperative that you gain an understanding of what this term means and how you can become competitor savvy – i.e. using your competitors to benefit your sales.

In your store, it is likely that you offer many products to sell. Lots of other businesses and retailers also distribute products which could be exactly the same or similar to yours. Being aware of exactly what your competitors sell and how they compare to what you sell in your store is called competitor analysis. It is literally analysing what your competition is selling and adjusting or adapting what you are selling or how you are selling it, accordingly, to ensure that you will not lose sales to your competition.

Customers these days are being communicated to through many different types of media and on many different levels. They are targeted through catalogues, tv, radio, newspapers, magazines and in more recent years, the internet and direct marketing via email. This makes most customers quite aware that competition can be fierce in retail, and many stores are competing against each other for their share of the marketplace.

Access to product information on the internet means that some customers will now be very knowledgeable about a product or a service before they even set foot in your store. They are also likely to know who else is selling that same product and for how much. As a salesperson, therefore, not only do you need to have excellent product knowledge about what you are selling, you also need to be well aware of who your direct competitors are and how much they are selling those products the same as yours for. It is very different to years gone by, where a customer was only guided by a catalogue or a simple tv or radio ad, and the information they were given by the salesperson.

The internet, perhaps more than any other medium, allows for a "push and pull" opportunity to market products, where customers are often targeted with unrequested emails about products or services, pushing them to buy. They are then supplied with internet sites to visit, making it extremely easy to learn more about products and services (and in the comfort of their own home or office), thereby more easily pulling them in to buy.

Know Your Competitors

It is a very competitive world that we live in now, no matter what sort of product you are selling. If you are working in a particularly competitive product environment, such as food, clothing or consumer goods, you need to be well aware of competitors in your local geographical region. A customer coming to you has assumingly also gone to your competitors as well. If you assume this, and know what sort of competition you are up against, you can negotiate your sale better with the customer, as you will know exactly what sort of price or condition that you have to beat or if you are already ahead of the competition.

Certain products are "destination products", meaning that a customer will come from far away or long distances for certain products if they stand out in their field - that is, if they are unique, hard to find, service a niche market etc. Most other products are not "destination products" and pose some serious competition amongst those retailers that sell them.

If you sell commodity items that are more readily available everywhere, then competition for sales will be stronger. It is very important, therefore, if you work in this type of environment to really be familiar with and understand your competitors' marketing strategies in your geographical region. Customers will sometimes use false statements relating to a like product offered by a competitor to try and get a better price from you. This is why you must be aware of your competitors, to stay on top of these situations.

With the ever growing number now too, of online suppliers of goods and services, there are even more competitors that are way beyond our geographical boundaries and present competition way beyond our control. Therefore, the awareness of the competition must be stronger than ever for you to be successful in securing and maintaining regular sales.

Techniques to Knowing Your Competitors

Whether you are in a retail store or working in an online store, the concept is the same regarding your competitors. You both need to be aware of each other's products and understand exactly where your competition lies. The products you sell, for example, could be wrapped in slightly different offerings by your competitors, making them either more or less of a threat to your products. Customers will often pick up on this and use this to get you to price match or offer them a better deal. Again, this is why you must be fully aware of exactly what your competition is offering, to know exactly what you are competing against.

Communication with other staff members and getting their views on who your direct competitors are is a good way to exchange information and learn from each other. This can be done in your regular meetings and handovers and is beneficial to the entire team. It is important to not only know who your competitors are, but what sort of prices they are offering; the quality of the product on offer, and how it compares to yours, too. Being familiar with who your online competitors are is also important, as now, more and more customers are experimenting with online shopping in preference to visiting physical stores.

Talking to management for their opinions regarding competitors – particularly online competitors - and what their counteracting strategies are to help you maintain your sales and increase your sales, will also be helpful and beneficial.

Here are some techniques that you could use to find out and keep up with who your competitors are:

- Go for regular walks in your mall or shopping strip to see what other businesses may be in direct competition with yours
- Use media such as newspapers and magazines to look at competitor's advertisements and special offers
- Read up on industry news to learn about new companies that may be launching products or services similar to yours

- Make note of any tv or radio advertising offering products or services that are in direct competition with yours
- Use the internet to research similar businesses or businesses selling similar products
- Talk to friends, family and colleagues to share information on what similar products or services are being offered that may be in direct competition to yours

Price Matching

Price matching is a common practice among retailers to enable them to retain a sale that they might otherwise lose to a competitor because the competitor is offering that same item at a cheaper price. After the competitor's price is verified by a copy of their advertisement or a phone call made directly to them at the point of sale, the higher price is overridden to match what the competitor was offering. Price matching is usually a win/win situation. It keeps the customer happy in that they are able to purchase what they want at the same, lower price as what the competition was offering, but it also helps the store to retain a customer who would have more than likely left to store to make their purchase with the competitor. Price matching shows good faith on the store's behalf and helps make the customer's experience in the store a positive one.

Usually there will be company policies regarding price matching set down by head office which are in place in your store. Often, you will need to clear price matching with management before you do it. It is also important to be aware of any government rulings that may surround price matching. If you are unable to match a competitor's price, you may have to concede to lose that sale but you can concentrate on something else that the customer may have also shown interest in and you may be successful in selling that item to your customer. There will also be times when perhaps you may pick up on sales at a later date of that item that you lost the sale on, as the competitor may run out of stock, or cease to offer the item at the reduced price that competed with yours.

Price Matching Pitfalls

One important factor that you need to be aware of when price matching, is that the product that are comparing prices on to possibly match, is exactly the same as what your store is offering – i.e. like the old saying: "you must compare apples with apples". The quality of the two products may vary, and factors like warranty period may differ. Sometimes, two competing stores will offer slightly different versions of a product – either slightly different models, or products packaged up with slightly different parts or accessories. Customers are not always clear on the differences and may only be focusing on the prices. You need to be aware of this to educate them on any distinct differences that may be the reason for the price variation to begin with, .before you agree to match the competitor's price.

For example, two stores may both offer a laptop package and be seen to be in direct competition with each other, with only the price that differs. This may not be the case, however. To demonstrate this, have a look at the following example of the laptop packages offered by the two competing stores.

In this example, overall, the packages look very similar, but the two packages differ very slightly in their content, with store B's laptop being slightly less powerful and with slightly different software included. In this case, store A could justify that the products are not identical and therefore, may choose not to price match.

STORE A's PACKAGE	STORE B's PACKAGE
Laptop: E7500 Processor, 250GB, 2GB RAM (DDR3), 250GB SATA hard drive, 13.3" screen, 3 year warranty	Laptop: E7500 Processor, 250GB, 2GB RAM (DDR), 170GB SATA hard drive, 13.3" screen, 3 year warranty
Targus carry bag	Targus carry bag
Software: WinXP Pro	Software: Windows 7.0,OfficePro
Total package price: $1,092.00	Total package price: $1,069.00

Minor variations like these can be easily overlooked by a customer wanting to price match. It is very important, therefore, that you are fully aware of exactly what is on offer by your competitors at all times. Today, too, there are a variety of specific websites dedicated to price matching. A lot of customers will be familiar with and refer to these, using them as bargaining tools to try and get a better deal. Together with online shopping, they help to provide time-saving, money-saving and effective shopping tools for customers, and need to be considered when considering whether or not to price match.

If you are really good at knowing what your competition is offering and when, you can sometimes use this to your advantage to secure a sale. When considering whether to buy or not, if you can educate your customer on the fact that what you are offering is currently cheaper than your competitor's version, or offers more advantages, this may help you to close the sale. To help you succeed, a simple practice like dedicating 30 minutes a week to researching competitors of products that you sell to be fully aware of where your competition lies, can prove very beneficial. You can even set up 'Google alerts' to help you! (www.google.com)

"If you want to win a race you have to go a little berserk!"

Bill Rodgers – American runner & former marathon record holder

ABOUT THE AUTHOR

Carlo Santoro was born and educated in Melbourne, Victoria, Australia. His business interests range from the retail industry, property market and the endless opportunities on the World Wide Web, to the commercial, political and aviation arenas.

Recognising a gap in the market some years back, Carlo facilitated the start-up of a successful company developing and managing operations and IT infrastructure for retailers – RetailCare. He maintains his role there today as Managing Director.

With more than fifteen years' experience in retail workings, Santoro spends the bulk of his time as an accomplished consultant and mentor to the retail industry. He also owns and has developed over 300 websites - many with on-line stores - and is constantly adding to this portfolio.

Carlo holds an MEI (Master of Entrepreneurship and Innovation) from Swinburne University and is recognised as one of the leading business networkers in Melbourne. Although his main focus lies with RetailCare, Carlo's extensive worldwide networks and expertise at business-to-business relationship building ensure that his business activities, like his enthusiasm for new ventures, remain dynamic.

Carlo places great importance on sharing knowledge and volunteering. He has held a prestigious leadership position for over 9 years with the Entrepreneurs' Organisation (EO) – an international non-profit organisation enabling groups of entrepreneurial business peers to meet and interact globally, growing and learning from each other along the way.

Outside of business Carlo is a dedicated father, living in Melbourne with his wife and two young children. He successfully juggles time with his many entrepreneurial ventures and time with his family.

Printed in Great Britain
by Amazon